# LETTERS TO
# SCATTERED PILGRIMS

# LETTERS TO
# SCATTERED PILGRIMS

*Elizabeth O'Connor*

1817

**HARPER & ROW, PUBLISHERS, San Francisco**
Cambridge, Hagerstown, New York, Philadelphia
London, Mexico City, São Paulo, Sydney

FIRST HARPER & ROW PAPERBACK EDITION
PUBLISHED 1982

---

**Library of Congress Cataloging in Publication Data**

O'Connor, Elizabeth.
    Letters to scattered pilgrims.

    1. Christian life—1960—    2. Church of the
Saviour, Washington, D.C.    I. Title.
BV4501.2.O317 1979    248'.4    78-3361
ISBN 0-06-066334-0

---

82 83 84 85 86    10 9 8 7 6 5 4 3 2 1

*To Agnes and Martin Gibbons, who have
made their home and hearts into a refuge
for wounded and aging men, and who have
modeled for their children and scores of
visitors what it means to be engaged
in building a society where the weak and
the strong are equally valued.*

# CONTENTS

*Foreword by Douglas V. Steere, ix*

*Preface, xiii*

*Acknowledgments, xvii*

*Lectionary, xix*

1 *On* Having Time for Reflection, *1*

2 *On* Money, *6*

3 *More on* Money, *14*

4 *On* Keeping a Journal, *31*

5 *On* the Journal and Group Life, *51*

6 *On* Our Multidimensional Nature, *64*

7 *On* Our Historical Center, *75*

8 *On* Our Intellectual Center, *83*

9 *On* Our Emotional Center, *95*

10 *On* Our Moving Center, *108*

11 *On* Children in the Wilderness, *132*

# *FOREWORD*

This innocent sounding title, *Letters to Scattered Pilgrims,* has a legitimate origin, for Elizabeth O'Connor did write these letters to stir and to nurture her pilgrim friends in the six new faith communities into which The Church of the Saviour has recently evolved. But do not be deceived by her ingenious device of these letters to the branches of her spiritual family into thinking that if you read them you can enjoy the luxury of sitting on the balcony and listening to someone else's frailties and family faults being almost shamelessly exposed. You will not get through many paragraphs before you will realize that "the enemy is me" and that, as in her other striking books, she has, in the course of telling the story of The Church of the Saviour's current concerns, succeeded in piercing her readers with a longing to get more deeply involved themselves.

In the early days of Pendle Hill, a Quaker study center in Philadelphia, we had a visit every year or two from Dorothy Day of the Catholic Worker. She had an uncanny way of beginning her talks by telling us that we Quakers had much too high an opinion of the Catholic Worker Movement. If we only knew them as she knew them, and knew herself among them, we should know what terrible frauds and hypocrites they really were, masquerading as people living in voluntary poverty when almost every one of them had some kind of nest egg or other that was still unsurrendered to God! Each further description of their frailties and disagreements and jealousies and reservations to letting go to the heart of things brought us at Pendle Hill lower and lower. For if *they* wore false masks that must all be surrendered when the midnight hour arrived, we were drawn to pray inwardly that God might have mercy on *us* who were so much further in arrears.

Elizabeth O'Connor's personal and group confessions that are sprinkled through these letters affect me much in the same way. Short of the Gospels, the letters on money in this little volume are as penetrating an analysis of the subject as I have ever seen, springing squarely out of the experiences of these faith communities.

In every letter, however, there is not only the sting of what it would mean if we took the Christian way seriously. There is also rich nurture and a readiness to take us as we are and to help move us on in. In this sense it is a workbook packed with the richest of anecdotes and passages from her wide reading that she longs to share with her readers, and with skillfully devised exercises that extend the thrust of her message. Her own insights have a luminous quality: "When all is said and done, the gift we have to give is to be authentic for each other," or a contemplative is "one who has been enough in the silence to be aware of his own poverty and lack of answers," or "we hurt when we are not thriving, loving creatures," or "where is the artist that has not had to battle as I do with enormous forces in themselves before things begin to flow," or "I think my strategy might be to gather into a small group a few young people from different parts of the world, to love them, to confirm their gifts, to listen to their conflicts and let them know that I am also a pilgrim in need of companions on the way."

Undergirding all of the letters is a basic premise that surfaces in her account of Baron Friedrich von Hügel's three elements that must be acknowledged and held in creative tension in all high religion. These three elements are: the mystical (emotional, experiential) element; the traditional (historical, social) element; and the intellectual (critical) element. If any element of this "multidimensional nature" of ours, as she refers to it, is ignored and the creative tension of these three factors is slacked, some form of low religion takes over. Dean Inge once noted that the greatest enemy of high religion is not irreligion but low religion.

Sane, balanced, searching, incisive, this book again confirms the judgment that in Elizabeth O'Connor, and in the remarkable community she so movingly interprets, we have a spiritual guide who is matched to the deepest needs of our time.

*Douglas V. Steere*
*Haverford College*

# PREFACE

Since its beginning in 1947, The Church of the Saviour in Washington, D.C., has been committed to the revolutionary concept of the priesthood of all believers. The church that takes that thought seriously must think of itself as a seminary to train laity for ministry in the world. A School of Christian Living has been basic to our own implementation of the Biblical teaching, "But you are *a chosen race, a royal priesthood, a consecrated nation, a people set apart . . .*" (1 Pet. 2:9 Jer.). The School's primary goal has been to help participants to exercise their gifts and to discover the work that each is born to do.

After persons have had two of the five classes required for full membership in the Church, they can become intern members of one of the small mission groups. The mission groups have two dimensions: a journey inward which includes an engagement with God, self and others, and a journey outward which includes an engagement with the world at a specific point of its need.

By 1975, the small mission groups, made up of five to twelve persons, were twenty-five in number. They were all thriving and engaged in many complex ministries. For example, the Jubilee mission group, concerned with housing for the poor, had purchased two apartment buildings and was renovating them for low income families. The people living in the buildings had become in a very real sense the mission's parish. Members were about the work of helping the tenants to discover their gifts, dream dreams, and have visions.

Other mission groups had taken on tasks equally large. It was no longer possible for the members to stay in close contact with each other. Communication was breaking down. We were faced with the choice of either adding staff members to hold the complex of mission groups together, or the more frightening alternative of separating into smaller administrative entities. The latter would place more responsibility upon laymen and laywomen, putting to a severe test the leadership training that had been a part of the community's life since its beginning. In spite of hesitations, fears and doubts, we made once again the decision to trust laypersons indeed to be ministers. To some it seemed that we were tossing everything in the air. To others we were obeying the injunction to cast the bread of our life upon the waters.

By the spring of 1976, The Church of the Saviour had reformed itself into six new church communities bearing the names:

The Dayspring Church

The Dunamis Vocations Church

The Eighth Day Church

The Jubilee Church

The Potter's House Church

The Seekers Church

The transition from one body into six separate bodies, each with its own leadership, worship, training, council and budget, was a time of immense uncertainty, sometimes anguish, for those involved. As in every passage, it was a time of crisis, carrying the possibility of death or of new life. We might have lost heart and returned to the known, only as with the Israelites there was no one to lead the way back, no Moses figure with the word of Yahweh in his mouth. The old had been forever lost, and the new did not yet exist in any important way. It was a time of anger, tears, complaints and disillusionment. It was a time of hoping, of planting seeds, forgiving, trusting, asking and watching, until the hidden light in each one's life became by day "the form of a pillar of cloud," and by night "the form of a pillar of fire" (Exod. 13:21 Jer.).

If we had known then what we know now, we probably could have made the transition without so much travail and so many groans. But such is not the way of life. Every individual, as well as every institution, must work out salvation in fear and trembling. When we avoid the anxiety and risk inherent in the new we turn from love and the One who said, "I have come so that they may have life and have it to the full" (John 10:10 Jer.).

During those months of Exodus, most of us were too concerned with our own futures to be good pastors to one another, but each in his own way and according to his own gifts did what was possible. Such was our "acting out" of the legend of the stone soup where each threw into the boiling water whatever she had and in the end there was nourishment for the whole village. When all is said and done the gift we have to give is to be authentic for each other. We dip into our own lives and offer what we find there. "I have neither silver nor gold, but I will give you what I have" (Acts 3:6 Jer.).

Every member was invited to contribute his or her favorite Scripture to become part of a lectionary that we could bind to our wrists as we travelled into the new land. Many in the congregation responded. Without eliminating a single offering we took the Scriptures and arranged them in chronological order, and had for the effort a Word from the Old Testament and a Word from the New Testament which seemed peculiarly appropriate for each week of the journey.

The letters in this volume are what I had to give to my sisters and brothers with whom I made this journey. The subjects were the ones that captured my attention as corporately we were forced to deal with issues of leadership, authority, separation, dependence and independence, and God's call, vision and forgiveness. The letters always turned into essays. With each one I promised that the next would be shorter, but every one had its own design and shape, and in the end I was the servant of a work rather than the creator.

The lectionary and letters are gathered together here for whatever help they may be for pilgrim persons all over the world, who are sensing God's call to the building of a more caring and just society. These pilgrim folk are aware that the promised land toward which they journey requires the conquest of inner territory, the disposition of inner pharaohs, and the establishment of one's own household under the Lordship of Christ.

As always a new book finds me in the debt of countless friends. I feel a deep gratitude for the generous and untiring editorial help of Dorothy Devers, who has worked with me on every book. Other special helpers in preparing this book were Mary Jo Cook, Harold Cary, Esther Dorsey, Conrad Hoover, Wes Michaelson, Jean Senseman, Pat Sitar, Don Foxvog, Sunny Branner and Alice Benson.

# ACKNOWLEDGMENTS

Grateful acknowledgment is made to the following for permission to reprint selections included in this book:

Mayfield Publishing Company for *Group Processes: An Introduction to Group Dynamics* by Joseph Luft. Copyright © 1963, 1970 Joseph Luft. See also *Of Human Interaction*.

Delacorte Press/Seymour Lawrence for excerpts from *God Bless You, Mr. Rosewater* by Kurt Vonnegut, Jr. Copyright © 1965 by Kurt Vonnegut, Jr.

Princeton University Press for excerpts from *A Short Life of Kierkegaard* by Walter Lowrie. Copyright © 1970 by Princeton University Press. pp. 235–237.

Viking Penguin Inc. for excerpts from *The Complete Short Stories of D. H. Lawrence*, Vol. III. Copyright 1933 by The Estate of D. H. Lawrence: Copyright © renewed 1961 Angelo Ravagli & C. M. Weekley, Executors of The Estate of Frieda Lawrence Ravagli.

New Directions Publishing Corp. for lines from "Blood of the Sun" in *The Collected Poems of Kenneth Patchen*. Copyright © 1945 by Kenneth Patchen.

# LECTIONARY

## FOR PILGRIMAGE TO THE NEW LAND

| | | |
|---|---|---|
| 1. Genesis 12 | Matthew 25 |
| 2. Genesis 22:1–18 | Luke 4 |
| 3. Exodus 2 | Luke 6:46–49 |
| 4. Exodus 3 | Luke 9:51–6- |
| 5. Exodus 16 | Luke 10:1–24 |
| 6. Exodus 19 | Luke 11:1–13 |
| 7. Numbers 13 | John 15 |
| 8. Numbers 14 | John 16:16–33 |
| 9. Deuteronomy 26:1–11 | John 17 |
| 10. Joshua 24 | Acts 4 |
| 11. I Kings 17:1–16 | Acts 5 |
| 12. Nehemiah 9:9–38 | Acts 6 |
| 13. Psalm 33 | Acts 7 |
| 14. Psalm 46 | Romans 8 |
| 15. Psalm 121 | Romans 12 |
| 16. Psalm 122 | 1 Corinthians 12 |
| 17. Psalm 127 | 1 Corinthians 13 |
| 18. Psalm 137 | Ephesians 1 |
| 19. Isaiah 6:1–13 | Ephesians 2 |
| 20. Isaiah 10:15, 11:11 | Ephesians 3 |
| 21. Isaiah 35 | Ephesians 4 |
| 22. Isaiah 42:18–43:4 | Ephesians 5 |
| 23. Isaiah 43:10–22 | Ephesians 6 |
| 24. Isaiah 52:13–53:12 | Philippians 1 |
| 25. Isaiah 55 | Philippians 2:1–18 |
| 26. Isaiah 62 | Galatians 5:13–25 |
| 27. Jeremiah 29:1–14 | Colossians 2:6–15 |
| 28. Jeremiah 31:31–40 | 1 John 1–2:11 |
| 29. Daniel 2:20–23 | 1John 3 |
| 30. Ezekiel 34 | 1 Peter 1:13–2:10 |
| 31. Amos 9:8–15 | 1 Peter 4 |
| 32. Micah 4:1–8 | Revelation 21 |
| 33. Micah 6:1–8 | Revelation 22 |

# 1

# ON
# HAVING TIME
# FOR REFLECTION

*Dear Brothers and Sisters:*

As some of you know, ten adults and four children in the Eighth Day Church have purchased a seven unit apartment building in the area of the Potter's House[1] and of our missions in the city. We are in the process of replacing most of our ceilings and walls, an undertaking that we had not planned.

One of my discoveries in recent years is that materials have a life. They also breathe and cease to breathe. Sometimes we keep our sheets and clothing long enough to know that they have lost their life. In the same way the plaster in our Eighth Day building is dead. Even when it appears all right, it is not all right. It sags and crumbles with any strong impact. The other day a friend mounting our stairs to the third floor was astounded to see a foot and leg hanging from the hall ceiling. On closer examination he discovered that they belonged to a member of the Eighth Day, who was in the attic investigating a leak in one of the apartments when he forged suddenly through floor and ceiling.

Because some of us are living in our apartments while we renovate them, we have gathered more information than we otherwise might have on how to make something look good on the outside though it is dying or dead underneath. The fact that we wanted our work to reflect an inner integrity heightened our awareness of the cosmetic kind of renovation that is being done for the poor all over this city, and for some unsuspecting rich. Such activity is tantamount to human beings preying on other human beings.

The imagery of Jesus sometimes addresses directly the matter of false appearances: "Alas for you, lawyers and Pharisees, hypocrites! You are like tombs covered with whitewash; they look well from outside, but inside they are full of dead men's bones and all kinds of filth" (Matt. 23:27–28 NEB). I think of these cosmetic renovations and of this Scripture as the members of our new faith communities struggle with their disciplines and articulate their visions for each other and for those who are yet unknown to us. So many of our statements are expressed in such lofty terms of a commitment to the oppressed that some of us wonder how we can translate them into our own lives and thus save ourselves from making hypocritical pronouncements.

Diego Irarrazaval C., speaking of the Chilean liberation struggle, said,

> . . .I want to clarify the basis of our reflection. We are coming to realize that the fundamental root of Christian thought is the question: What is to be done? This is not a doctrinal question like: What do we believe? Nor is it a moral question we raise: How are we to do good?
>
> Given our commitment to those who suffer most and who have the greatest right to head the liberation process, the question, *What is to be done?* reads more like an ultimatum! We Christians invented neither the question nor the answer. The concrete and actual protagonists of the revolutionary process are those who pose the question. It is the oppressed who demand of us a response, who challenge all Christians who are neither "hot nor cold."[2]

I have wondered about the relationship of the Sabbath to that all important question as I have hurried home from church on Sunday to work in my apartment. I am sometimes overwhelmed by what has to be done so that order and grace can come into my rooms. Sunday afternoon is a fine time for hard labor that will move me toward my goal. I would like to think that this is a special situation, but the fact is that I have never kept the Sabbath. I don't believe that anyone in the whole Church of the Saviour community does very well at keeping the Sabbath. It may be the day that we work the hardest.

I have thought about this in a deeper way since reading Dr. Wilfried Daim's commentary on the Fourth Commandment, "Remember to keep the sabbath day holy. You have six days to labour and do all your work" (Exod. 20:8–9 NEB):

> Moses' Fourth Commandment is the first law in history to protect man's free time. It even protected domestic animals, not merely women and servants, against exploitation. This law did not place too heavy a strain on the labor supply of a society whose productive capacity was incomparably lower than today's. The modern struggle for the eight-hour day cannot compare in importance with the institution of one free day in the week. In the Decalogue, the Fourth Commandment is nearly as important as the first.
>
> The free time legislated in the Fourth Commandment has retained its function to this day. It is a time to face God, or, in secular terms, to recall life's meaning, to concentrate on cultivation of one's humanity, and to catch one's breath: "For on the seventh day, God caught his breath," as the Biblical passage should properly be translated.[3]

As I type those words I think to myself that I will begin keeping the Fourth Commandment when I have created some order in which to dwell. But another part of me responds: *What will you have gained, if the order on the outside does not have a corresponding inner order?* In Scripture a person's own being is the house. The rooms to be prepared for the coming of a Presence are inward ones. The door to be opened requires that the householder be at home. We can always find a good reason for not keeping the Sabbath—always choose or accept the imposition of new deadlines, moving from one deadline to the next, hurrying through all the days of the week, so that we can hurry through the seventh. What if Moses had said to the children of Israel, "Our lives are endangered. We cannot rest until we are more certain of survival, but once we make it safely into the New Land, we will begin keeping the Sabbath. Then we can begin to reflect on our week and look to God for direction."

I live in a community of God's people, but we are often too

busy to be with each other. In little spaces we attempt to deal with the injustices of the world, and the questions that they pose: *What is to be done?* We sometimes say to each other that we are looking forward to the time when we will have leisure to be together, forgetting what every wise one knows—that the way to a goal can change the goal.

This morning I paused again over these Scriptures and their meaning for our new faith communities and for pilgrims everywhere.

> If you cease to tread the sabbath
>     underfoot,
> and keep my holy day free from
>     your own affairs,
>         if you call the sabbath a day of joy
> and the Lord's holy day a day to be
>     honoured,
> if you honour it by not plying
>     your trade,
> not seeking your own interest
> or attending to your own affairs,
> then you shall find your joy in the
>     Lord,
> and I will set you riding on the heights
>     of the earth .... (Isa. 58:13–14 NEB)

Of course a decision to keep the Sabbath can become another heavy rule to give us a long-faced look, or it can be a means of liberation—freeing us from all the deadlines that we are always making for ourselves and for each other. Perhaps on the Sabbath we can find time to be with each other, to listen to each other and care for each other. If we give ourselves permission not to bake, or mow the lawn, or shop on the Sabbath, perhaps we can learn to be present to each other and create our heaven right now, straighten out our priorities and join the revolution because we have had time to deal with the question of "What is to be done?"

When I think about how I might keep the Fourth Commandment I can understand how our fathers arrived at over 400 rules about what could and could not be done on the Sabbath. And yet one needs guidelines. I think I shall practice reserving my own Sabbath for reflection and prayer, the writing of notes, and the visiting of the ill.

I shall also eat with my friends on that day and invite them to eat with me, but I shall do no preparation of food, no shopping, no cleaning on that holy day. All of that will have to be done before or not at all. I think that I shall also visit friends in other faith communities and give encouragement and ask for it. I am hoping that some of you will decide to keep the Sabbath so that you will greet my coming, and not find it an intrusion upon your work—so that we can support each other and discover whether the keeping of this commandment enhances life and enables us to exult in life as the Scripture promises. Perhaps together we can recover the meaning of the seventh day so that it can become "a day of joy."

*Elizabeth*

## NOTES

1. The coffee house operated by the Potter's House Church.
2. "What Is to Be Done? Christians in the Socialist Process," a speech given November 25, 1972.
3. "The First Revolutionary," *The Center Magazine* (September/October 1972), p. 45.

# 2

# ON
# MONEY

*Dear Sisters and Brothers:*

"Filthy lucre," as money is sometimes called, has been a favorite topic of conversation for us since the early days of The Church of the Saviour. We talk about it probably as much as Jesus did. When the founding members, young and poor, were forming themselves into a properly incorporated community of faith, they struggled for a discipline of membership that would help them and future members to deal concretely with at least some aspects of the handling of money. In its first writing the discipline read, "We commit ourselves to giving 10 percent of our gross income to the work of the Church."

While there was some precedence in biblical history for the 10 percent figure, our first members felt that this kind of giving would enable them to begin to tackle the injustices of society in a way that would be meaningful to themselves, as well as to others. Their proposed constitution and disciplines were submitted to Reinhold Niebuhr, an eminent theologian of the last generation, who had agreed to read them and comment. His only suggestion concerned the discipline on money. "I would suggest," Niebuhr said, "that you commit yourselves not to tithing but to proportionate giving, with tithing as an economic floor beneath which you will not go unless there are some compelling reasons." The discipline was rewritten and stands today in each of the six new faith communities:

We covenant with Christ and one another to give proportionately beginning with a tithe of our incomes.

None of us has to be an accountant to know what 10 percent of a gross income is, but each of us has to be a person on his knees before God if we are to understand our commitment to proportionate giving. Proportionate to what? Proportionate to the accumulated wealth of one's family? Proportionate to one's income and the demands upon it, which vary from family to family? Proportionate to one's sense of security and the degree of anxiety with which one lives? Proportionate to the keenness of our awareness of those who suffer? Proportionate to our sense of justice and of God's ownership of all wealth? Proportionate to our sense of stewardship for those who follow after us? And so on, and so forth. The answer, of course, is in proportion to all of these things.

Proportionate giving has kept us from mistaking our churchgoing for Christianity, and from looking at our neighbor to see what we should be doing. In our better moments we desire that each member and intern member work under the guidance of the Holy Spirit to determine what proportionate giving means in his or her individual situation. We have, of course, hoped for ourselves and for others that the proportion of giving would increase as we identified with the oppressed and learned to trust God at deeper levels for our own futures.

By and large the discipline has served us well. Over the years we have kept the 10 percent floor for members and the 5 percent floor for our intern members. Many have struggled with the minimum giving, and some have turned away. Others have broken loose and showered our community with riches. The borders of the mission have been pushed out, and the suffering of our city has been eased a bit. Sometimes the giving has been excessive and ecstatic, and sometimes impulsive—a diamond engagement ring dropped in the offering plate, a silver service set appearing at the door, a check for several thousand dollars representing the total accumulated wealth of a young couple.

I first heard the tithing discipline explained in a class in Christian Growth that I was taking when I was new to The Church of the Saviour and the Christian faith. Following the class we met with the members of other classes for a short worship service. The small chapel rang with the words, "Blessed be the tie that binds our hearts in Christian love." My untutored ears heard the words as "Blessed be the tithe. . . ." I went home to explain the discipline to my non-religious household, and commented, "They even sing about it."

The next Sunday we all went to see those strange people, and to hear about the things they were planning. Gordon Cosby was preaching his annual sermon on money, which was as spellbinding then as now. Before the year was over my household was tithing, and when the time came to purchase a retreat farm, we threw caution to the wind and went with everyone else to borrow what we could toward the down payment. It was not that our souls were so quickly converted, but that we sensed that something important was going on, and we wanted to be a part of it. We had been captured by a man's vision of what a community might do if it really cared about the oppressed and the suffering.

In a recent sermon on money Gordon said as forcefully as ever that to give away money is to win a victory over the dark powers that oppress us. He talked about reclaiming for ourselves the energy with which we have endowed money:

> I think we need to grapple with the place of money in our lives at a level which is more profound than ever before. We are caught in the order of necessity and death—the order of the Gentiles who worry about what they eat and what they drink and what they wear— the order of nature since the fall—the order that is unto death. We must break the chains of this order. We must give lavishly and cheerfully, else we die.
>
> I am not interested in raising a budget. If we had no budget at all it would be tremendously important for us to look at money, and how it relates to the Christian faith and to our life. Money is a hangup for many of us. We will not be able to advance in the Christian faith until we have dealt at another level with the material. It is a matter of understanding what it means to be faithful to Jesus Christ.

He went on to say that the poor suffer because they are not able to give, as well as because they lack enough of the necessities of life. He told how he had learned this "the hard way":

I was the minister of a small Baptist congregation in a railroad town just outside of Lynchburg, Virginia. My deacon sent for me one day and told me that he wanted my help. "We have in our congregation." he said, "a widow with six children. I have looked at the records and discovered that she is putting into the treasury of the church each month $4.00—a tithe of her income. Of course, she is unable to do this. We want you to go and talk to her and let her know that she needs to feel no obligation whatsoever, and free her from the responsibility."

I am not wise now; I was less wise then. I went and told her of the concern of the deacons. I told her as graciously and as supportively as I knew how that she was relieved of the responsibility of giving. As I talked with her the tears came into her eyes. "I want to tell you," she said, "that you are taking away the last thing that gives my life dignity and meaning."

I tried to retrieve the situation. I was unable to do it. I went home and pondered the story of Jesus in the temple watching the people put their offerings in the collection plate. Jesus' attitude amazed me. He had the audacity to watch what people were putting in the collection. Not only did he have the audacity to watch, he had the audacity to comment. Of the rich who put in large sums he said, "They put in what they can easily afford." Of the poor widow who dropped in two coins, he said, "She in her poverty, who needs so much, has given away everything, her whole living." I asked myself—"What would I have done?" I knew. I would have said to her, "Let us take this to the council. We have a sensible council that always makes exceptions and I know that they will relieve you of your discipline of giving."

Without any doubt Gordon's teaching-sermons on money have influenced the whole orientation of the new communities toward the material area of life. Each of them began on a sound financial basis because each began with a small nucleus of tithing members. All contributions to the communities are used to further the work of the missions within the year they are given. Nothing has ever been put aside for a rainy day. We have followed faithfully the injunction given by Moses to his people as he led them out of bondage, "No one must keep any of it for tomorrow" (Exod. 16:19 Jer.).

Despite our corporate style and our exposure to the issues that are raised around the subject of money, we know that we have not gained much "downward mobility." While we have succeeded in stabilizing our standard of living, most of us cling to what we have known. Though the budgets of our faith communities are large by traditional standards, we are fully aware that they represent only a fraction of the potential giving of the congregation.

We still wrestle with fear when we consider abandoned giving. Our wills, with rare exceptions, look like the wills of those who have never been committed to the building of a faith community, or who have never had the poor in mind. This may indicate that, in the face of the threat caused by the consideration of our deaths, we regress to old definitions of family and narrower spheres of identity. In any case, most of us would probably say that we are not as free as we would like to be where the material things of life are concerned. What may have looked like radical obedience to us a quarter of a century ago, no longer seems radical today. Coming to know some of our suffering sisters and brothers in the Third World and in the ghettoes of Washington has made all the difference in the way we view the earth. The unemployment statistics are made up of faces that we know. We behold the plight of the poor not only with fresh eyes, but with the awareness that our faithfulness in the past gave God one way of performing veritable miracles. Scattered throughout our new faith communities are persons who ask with increasing uneasiness what it means to be faithful at this time in their individual treks and in our slow migration as a people out of the old orders of "necessity and death." In a personal and in a corporate way we are wrestling once more with the question of what we are to do with our money. Some of us experience an inner division, for our hearts so often tell us one thing and our heads another. When we begin to take the Scriptures seriously, "You cannot serve God and Money" (Matt. 6:24 NEB) becomes a personal address. One would expect God to applaud our small efforts at faithfulness; instead a Spirit comes and takes us where we are not yet prepared to go.

Father Leo Mahon, who describes the Old and New Testaments as the "How to Be a Great People" book, once said:

> You can't read the Word of God! The Word of God is not in a book. The key to the Word of God is in the book, but the Word of God is in life. You've got to know the Word of God, and "know" in Scripture means love and enter into. So it is only when we enter into life in our society and feel with other people and hurt with them that the Word of God can occur.[1]

That is a very simple and very profound statement. As we become exposed to the poor and their needs, the rich young ruler and the widow and her mite lose the storybook quality of our childhood faith, and become figures in the counterculture literature of a revolutionary leader—the very one whom we call Saviour. The First Commandment and all the Scriptures on the worship of idols begin to lay bare our own primitive selves. Some of us have looked into the face of our idols and found that one of them is money.

Though we along with millions of other churchgoers are saying that Jesus saves, we ask ourselves if we are not in practice acting as though it were money that saves. We say that money gives power, money corrupts, money talks. Like the ancients with their molten calf we have endowed money with our own psychic energy, given it arms and legs, and have told ourselves that it can work for us. More than this we enshrine it in a secret place, give it a heart and a mind and the power to grant us peace and mercy.

The issue of money was also raised for us in the financing of our missions. Should we make a concerted drive to win foundation support and government grants for our projects in the inner city? Was such a path a model for the revolution that we were reading about in Scripture? Would it put us in the position of having to say to the churches who were inquiring about the financing of our inner city work, "You begin by securing a list of the foundations and then choose the ones you will go after. This means coming to know the people who have control of large sums of money. If you are successful in your pastoring/propheting relationship, they will give you their money, even if they do not join you in your mission." Was this the way of

Christ? Did he say to the rich young ruler, "The movement needs your money," or "We need you, and it looks as though the money will be in the way. Sell what you have. Give it to the poor and when you have grown rich in the things of the spirit, come be a part of the mission."

We know that in the early days of Koinonia Farm when the community was beginning a program to provide modest dwellings for destitute people in the surrounding area, Clarence Jordan, the founder and spiritual leader, told a wealthy woman who was interested in joining Koinonia that she would have to dispose of her money to become a part of them.

> "How?" she asked. "Give it to the poor," he said. "Give it to your relatives, throw it over a bridge—but you must enter the fellowship without it." "What about giving it to Koinonia Farm?" she asked.
> Clarence grinned, and replied: "No. If you put that money in here several things would happen. First of all, we'd quit growing peanuts and start discussing theology. That wouldn't be a healthy condition for us. And in the next place, unless I miss my guess you are a very lonely person, and you are lonely because you think every friend you ever had is after your money."
> She confirmed that judgment.
> "Well," Clarence continued, "If you put that money in here, you would think we courted you for your money, that we loved you for your money. And in the next place, if you put that money in here you would get the idea you were God's guardian angel, that you endowed the rest of us, and that all of us ought to be grateful to you for your beneficence.... Now for your sake and for our sake, you get rid of that money and come walk this way with us."[2]

Do we believe with Clarence Jordan that money and possessions have a way of coming between people who want to be in community with each other? Do we really believe that every life has resources more priceless than gold, and that our hearts, minds and labor are adequate for any task? What if the world is right and there are things that only money can buy, gifts of the spirit that only money can unlock, and blocks that only money can push aside?

The questions continue to be raised, and we continue to struggle for the answers that in the end have to be individual answers, for we are each at a different place in our spiritual trek with different understandings of what the Gospel has to say to us about what we do with our money.

*Elizabeth*

## NOTES

1. Speech, Sept. 25, 1974, by Rev. Leo Mahon, Pastor, St. Victor Parish, Calumet City, Illinois.
2. Dallas Lee, *The Cotton Patch Evidence* (New York: Association Press, 1971), pp. 86–87.

# 3

# MORE
# ON MONEY

*Dear Brothers and Sisters:*

Reflecting again on money, I thought it might be helpful for all of us to known how the subject is being worked with in various segments of the Church. Sometimes we can helpfully adopt what another community is doing; even when this is not the case another's effort can stimulate our imaginations and suggest ways for us to move. After all, we have the injunction to stir one another to good works.

The Wellspring Workshops on money come especially to mind as a possible design for a weekend retreat. As you know, Don McClanen (the founder of Wellspring[1]) is fearless about taking this emotionally charged topic out of the closet. For the first workshop on the fateful subject, I was part of the leadership, which included Don, Chris Raible, minister of the First Unitarian Church, Worcester, Massachusetts, and Fred Taylor, one of the co-pastors of our Seekers Church. In our own individual ways each of us was a student of the subject of money. In reflecting on our histories we found that our decisions and attitudes toward money had been shaped by (1) our childhood homes and early experiences, (2) by the church, and (3) by society. While we agreed that the three forces of past, church and society often overlapped and were congenial with each other, we also found that the voices from these three impacting areas were sometimes in conflict. The conference was designed to help us explore all three spheres of influence.

In the course of the weekend participants shared their expectations, hopes and, once in a great while, their fears. We pondered Scriptures on money and used journal exercises to reach back to discover what home and parents had taught us about money. We played games with money to be in touch with more instinctive responses to our handling of it; in pairs we shared our happiest and saddest experience with money, an exercise that I would especially recommend to you. We worked with some of the literature on money, and took time to study and behold the dollar bill with its forgotten symbols and messages —so beautifully succinct and so ideal: the phrase, "In God We Trust," and the image of God's eye, perhaps intended for a reminder that the Spirit of the Lord is aware of what all humankind says and does. Did the makers of the dollar bill hope that in our giving and receiving of this note we would be reminded of eternal truths and claims and not mistake it for the Almighty?

Around the theme of money we worshipped, sang and danced.

> Ho, every one who thirsts,
>     come to the waters:
> and he who has no money,
>     come, buy and eat!
> Why do you spend your money for that
>     which is not bread,
> and your labor for that which does not
>     satisfy?                    (Isa. 55:1–2 RSV)

We worked with a financial inventory that would give us an understanding of what our resources were. A few discovered how vague they liked to keep the matter of just how much they had. While it caused a certain amount of anxiety, it might cause them more anxiety to discover that they were, indeed, rich. While most of us probably would have said that our attitude toward money had not changed very much, we found that where the possession of a little wealth would have once added to our

self-esteem, it now caused uneasiness. We longed for the freedom of that man in Christ who said:

> I have learned to manage on whatever I have, I know how to be
> poor and I know how to be rich too. I have been through my initia-
> tion and now I am ready for anything anywhere: full stomach or
> empty stomach, poverty or plenty.          (Phil. 4:11–13 Jer.)

We each wrote a letter to ourselves that Chris Raible agreed
to mail to us in three months. In mine was a list of things I would
do, such as, "Think about the needs of your old age. Does the
'rainy day' have to be kept in mind as cautious voices instruct?
I am beginning to have my doubts. Louise Smith, who for many
years has been responsible for maintaining the beauty and the
order of the Old Victorian mansion in which the new communities had their beginning, told me in a conversation the other
day that her husband had sufficient money for her to be in the
very best of retirement or nursing homes, if that became necessary. "But," she said, "I have no intentions of going to any of
them. I want to be where the people are poor and need me." I
asked her what made her think she, herself, would not be feeble
and in need? "I meant," she said, "where they will need my
spirit." As we talked Gordon Cosby came in. I shared Louise's
plan for the future with him. He thought he might like to spend
his closing years in prison, though he was uncertain about how
that might be accomplished.

The fact that both of them saw themselves performing in old
age the ministry that they had been committed to all their lives
caused me to pause. I wondered why I had imagined myself in
need of help, deserted and alone, depressed by the absence of
friends and deprived of work. Louise and Gordon pictured
themselves in the midst of people, continuing their ministry.
On reflection, it seemed to me that what they envisioned for
themselves was very likely to be realized for visions often seem
empowered toward fulfillment. I have begun to live with a new
image of my future, an image of love rather than of fear.

In my letter to myself I also put a notation to "think about why
it is that some people who have chosen an austere life-style
sound so self-righteous." I have wondered if these folk are not
a little miserable with their decision. They remind me that giv-

ing away money and "doing good" do not give us detachment. That requires another kind of work. We must all determine for ourselves what that work is and begin doing it. Perhaps Carl Jung gave us a clue when he said that if we continue to feel poor when we have enough of the world's goods, it is because we have not given sufficient attention to the claims of the inner person.

During the conference many found the times of worship and Bible study healing the division within themselves, and the thought leaped up that we might have dispensed with all the intellectualizing and all the talking about money, and simply given ourselves to prayer and worship. After all, maybe God would save, if properly petitioned. As true as that may turn out to be, we concluded that our grappling for truth had focused our prayer and worship and left us a little more open to God's word. At one point in the worship we considered an "if only..." that was draining our energy. We wrote our "if only..." on a slip of paper and dropped it in the log fire, and watched regret burn away. If indeed that did happen it was because the confession on the slip had grown out of a "facing up" to a truth about ourselves. Guilt clings to us because forgiveness is pronounced over things not very close to our real pain. Why we are anxious is not an easy discovery to make.

In the course of the conference Chris Raible read from two publications. They are lengthy readings to include in a letter. I do so because of an irresistible urge to place in another's hands what has moved me. The first was from "The Rocking Horse Winner"[2] by D. H. Lawrence:

> There were a boy and two little girls. They lived in a pleasant house, with a garden, and they had discreet servants, and felt themselves superior to anyone in the neighborhood.
>
> Although they lived in style, they felt always an anxiety in the house. There was never enough money. The mother had a small income, and the father had a small income, but not nearly enough for the social position which they had to keep up. The father went into town to some office. But though he had good prospects, these prospects never materialized. There was always the grinding sense of the shortage of money, though the style was always kept up.
>
> At last the mother said: "I will see if I can't make something." But

she did not know where to begin. She racked her brains, and tried this thing, and the other, but could not find anything successful. The failure made deep lines come into her face. Her children were growing up, they would have to go to school. There must be more money, there must be more money. The father, who was always very handsome and expensive in his tastes, seemed as if he never *would* be able to do anything worth doing. And the mother, who had a great belief in herself, did not succeed any better, and her tastes were just as expensive.

And so the house came to be haunted by the unspoken phrase: *There must be more money. There must be more money.* The children could hear it all the time, though nobody said it aloud. They heard it at Christmas, when the expensive and splendid toys filled the nursery. Behind the shining modern rocking-horse, behind the smart doll's house, a voice would start whispering: "There must be more money. There *must* be more money." The children could hear it all the time, though nobody said it aloud. And the children would stop playing, to listen, for a moment. They would look into each other's eyes, to see if they had all heard. And each one saw in the eyes of the other two that they too had heard. "There *must* be more money. There *must* be more money."

It came whispering from the springs of the still-swaying rocking horse, and even the horse, bending his wooden, champing head, heard it. The big doll, sitting so pink and smirking in her new pram, could hear it quite plainly, and seemed to be smirking all the more self-consciously because of it. The foolish puppy, too, that took the place of the teddybear, he was looking so extraordinarily foolish for no other reason but that he heard the secret whisper all over the house: "There *must* be more money."

Yet nobody ever said it aloud. The whisper was everywhere, and therefore no one spoke it. Just as no one ever says: "We are breathing," in spite of the fact that breath is coming and going all the time.

The words were sad and arresting. They took us back to the rooms of our parents to listen to the whispers there. Some heard, "We must not touch the capital. You know, we must *never* touch the capital. You may not touch the capital." Long before the child knew what capital meant, he had the message that to touch it was to die. "You cannot see my face . . . for man cannot see me and live" (Exod. 33:20 Jer.).

The next day I rushed to the library and found the paperback copy of Volume Three of *The Complete Short Stories of D. H. Law-*

*rence* and read "The Rocking Horse Winner." Lawrence does what every true artist does—puts us in touch with ourselves—our thoughts and feelings and hollow places. My expedition to the library returned me to the world of poems and stories that had nurtured my early life. Somehow along the way I had given up reading them, mistakenly feeling that nonfiction had more to tell me about reality.

At our workshop the second reading was from another work of fiction—*God Bless You, Mr. Rosewater*[3] by Kurt Vonnegut, Jr.:

"Eliot—"

"Sir—?"

"We come to a supremely ironic moment in history, for Senator Rosewater of Indiana now asked his own son, 'Are you or have you ever been a communist?' "

"Oh, I have what a lot of people would probably call communistic thoughts," said Eliot artlessly, "but, for heaven's sakes, Father, nobody can work with the poor and not fall over Karl Marx from time to time—or just fall over the Bible, as far as that goes. I think it's terrible the way people don't share things in this country. I think it's a heartless government that will let one baby be born owning a big piece of the country, the way I was born, and let another baby be born without owning anything. The least a government could do, it seems to me, is to divide things up fairly among the babies. Life is hard enough, without people having to worry themselves sick about money, too. There's plenty for everybody in this country, if we'll only share more."

"And just what do you think that would do to incentive?"

"You mean fright about not getting enough to eat, about not being able to pay the doctor, about not being able to give your family nice clothes, a safe, cheerful, comfortable place to live, a decent education, and a few good times? You mean shame about not knowing where the Money River is?"

"The what?"

"The Money River, where the wealth of the nation flows. We were born on the banks of it—and so were most of the mediocre people we grew up with, went to private schools with, sailed and played tennis with. We can slurp from that mighty river to our hearts' content. And we even take slurping lessons, so we can slurp more efficiently."

"Slurping lessons?"

"From lawyers! From tax consultants! From customers' men!

We're born close enough to the river to drown ourselves and the next ten generations in wealth, simply using dippers and buckets. But we still hire the experts to teach us the use of aqueducts, dams, reservoirs, siphons, bucket brigades, and the Archimedes' screw. And our teachers in turn become rich, and their children become buyers of lessons in slurping."

"I wasn't aware that I slurped."

Eliot was fleetingly heartless, for he was thinking angrily in the abstract. "Born slurpers never are. And they can't imagine what the poor people are talking about when they say they hear somebody slurping. They don't even know what it means when somebody mentions the Money River. When one of us claims that there is no such thing as the Money River I think to myself, 'My gosh, but that's a dishonest and tasteless thing to say.' "

"If there isn't a Money River, then how did I make ten thousand dollars today, just by snoozing and scratching myself, and occasionally answering the phone?"

"It's still possible for an American to make a fortune on his own."

"Sure—provided somebody tells him when he's young enough that there is a Money River, that there's nothing fair about it, that he had damn well better forget about hard work and the merit system and honesty and all that crap, and get to where the river is. 'Go where the rich and the powerful are,' I'd tell him, 'and learn their ways. They can be flattered and they can be scared. Please them enormously or scare them enormously, and one moonless night they put their fingers to their lips, warning you not to make a sound. And they will lead you through the dark to the widest, deepest river of wealth ever known to man. You'll be shown your place on the river bank, and handed a bucket all your own. Slurp as much as you want, but try to keep the racket of your slurping down. A poor man might hear!' "

The two readings received very little space in our conference, but they gave us distance from ourselves so that we could observe the one in us who would like to be immersed in the river of wealth where all desires are met and all wishes come true. Of course discerning greed in ourselves is no easy accomplishment, since it is wounding to self-esteem to discover in one's own responses what we condemn in others. Who likes to give up the image of himself as a caring, generous person unhampered by the money hang-ups that plague his friends? More disturbing yet is the awakening recognition of the injustice of one's own privileged position. For me to rage against greedy industrialists or biased lawmakers is one thing. To search for the truth that runs contrary to personal ambitions and wishes is quite another.

We spoke rarely about the people who have no work or too little to eat, though our awareness of them had led us into an examination of the role of money in our own lives. We had begun to see the connection between the way people ordinarily relate to money, and all the misery and oppression in the world. Some of us were reading Deuteronomy and finding it a document full of mercy, justice and care for the weak. Were these laws upon our hearts?

If you are making your fellow a loan on pledge, you are not to go into his house and seize the pledge, whatever it may be. You must stay outside, and the man to whom you are making the loan shall bring the pledge out to you. And if the man is poor, you are not to go to bed with his pledge in your possession; you must return it to him at sunset so that he can sleep in his cloak and bless you; and it will be a good action on your part in the sight of Yahweh your God.                                                   (Deut. 24:10–15 Jer.).

You are not to exploit the hired servant who is poor and destitute, whether he is one of your brothers or a stranger who lives in your towns. You must pay him his wage each day, not allowing the sun to set before you do, for he is poor and is anxious for it; otherwise he may appeal to Yahweh against you, and it would be a sin for you.
(Deut. 24:14–15 Jer.)

When you harvest your vineyard you must not pick it over a second time. Let anything left be for the stranger, the orphan and the widow.

Remember that you were a slave in the land of Egypt. That is why I lay this charge on you.                                   (Deut. 24:21–22 Jer.)

What do we do with these words from Isaiah?

Woe to those who add house to house and join field to field until everywhere belongs to them. . . .                                (Isa. 5:8 Jer.)

While the Wellspring Workshops are raising for pilgrim persons the seriousness of biblical teachings on money, the Sojourners[4] community is working with these same teachings on the streets of the inner city. As I write this, several friends from

Sojourners are in that hell hole which is our district jail. It was not in their planning to be there. They had articles to write and children to cradle, speeches to give and walks to take, when a woman came to them asking help for herself and children who were threatened with eviction. She was a woman who worshipped with the Sojourners on Sunday mornings. They had told her in songs and litany and prayers that she was their sister and that they were all members of God's household and that nobody need be afraid. Now she had come with her trouble as anyone's sister would, and they had listened as families do.

The more they listened the more involved they became until they found themselves talking to a teacher of law at a nearby religious institution. Together with another person he had bought the five-unit house in which the woman lived. They told the teacher that the people in his apartments were poor people with no place in the city to go. They explained the suffering that had been caused by real estate speculation in the area, and about the Land Trust that religious groups had established to take houses off the market and make them available to poor people. Finally they offered to pay him the $50,000 that he had paid for the apartment house plus all the expenses he had incurred.

The teacher of law did not find this at all reasonable. If he rid his building of the tenants and let it stand vacant for six months, the law would place no limits on the profits. Old apartments in the inner city are worth considerably more without tenants, and he planned to list it for $90,000. He did not seem to remember the land of Egypt, or that he had ever been a slave or a stranger. He could only think about the calf of gold that was installed in the empty place inside himself.

Three of the five apartment units had already been vacated and he wanted the other occupants to move without "causing any trouble." He knew how to use the law to accomplish this and within the days prescribed by that law he served the woman and her neighbors the papers announcing their eviction date. They had no place to go and the Sojourners had no space to offer to them, so they said what friends will always say to distressed friends, "Do not be afraid. We will be with you." This is how three of them happened to be in the building and why in the morning the police came and why they were arrested.

The police were sympathetic but, in the end, shrugged their shoulders and said, "It is all a matter of money." That was clear to everyone—the neighbors up and down the street, the judge, the newspapers, the teacher of law, and the community at prayer —it is a matter of money.

I believe with Lord Byron that "Long communion tends to make us what we are."[5] I want to commune with men and women who are further along in the "conscientization"[6] process than I am. I want to be seared by their words and experiences until I lose my fear of finding myself fighting at their side. I am not afraid that their statements will make me feel guilty. Guilt can be neurotic, but guilt can also let us know when we are injuring ourselves or injuring others. It comes to restore us to ourselves and to move us toward relationship with the earth and all that is thereon. It becomes destructive when we do not hear its message.

As for our money, we would usually rather keep the vague, uneasy feelings we have about it than do something foolish like giving some of it away. Even when that absurd thought does linger with us we lack the motivation for any decisive step in that direction. We have no close friends among the poor. We rarely draw near enough to hear their outcries. As we pay for our own bags of groceries, we may wonder "how the poor manage these days," but the thought is fleeting and does not keep us awake at night. When the harsh sound and sight of poverty intrude upon our ears and eyes, we try to wipe out the memory—to "think of something pleasant." As a result we blunt our sensitivity and dull our capacity to see and hear not only what is disturbing or ugly, but also what is quieting or beautiful.

We do not choose to do anything very much about the misery in the world because we are not in any real sense aware of it. We read about it and hear about it, but the existence of poverty has no effect on our emotional life. We would not know how to go about drawing close to the poor, even if we wanted that experience. Furthermore, we are inclined to ask what difference it would make. In the face of the overwhelming need of the world's destitute, what can individuals do except feel their own helplessness?

As Wellspring and the Sojourners, each in their own way, worked with the issue of money, the Dunamis Vocations Church (one of the six faith communities of The Church of the Saviour) began addressing a similar question: How can we open the structures of society—and our own lives—to feel the hurts of the dispossessed. Dunamis is a Greek word used in the New Testament to designate the power promised to the disciples to enable them to witness to the ends of the earth. Members of the church have covenanted with one another to bring Christ into the arena of their vocations, and to hold each other accountable for consciously struggling to transform their places of work into communities of caring that enable life and growth in people.

The leaders of the new job-oriented church are a school teacher, a clinical psychologist, a social worker and a librarian. They are encouraging in the hearts and minds of their small flock the astonishing thought that each of them can receive every day the power to turn classrooms, government agencies and institutions into places where love is nourished and justice done. The young church attempts to maintain not only a prophetic role toward those in positions of power, but also a pastoral role.

As members developed strong relationships with persons of authority and influence they began to think more about the education of their own emotional and sensory life in relationship to the poor. They felt they were trying to be a voice for the poor without knowing them in any real sense. As their journey inward to know God had once needed a corresponding outward journey of engagement with the world, now their journey upward into spheres of power required the balance of a journey downward to be with the powerless.

Unsure of a way to accomplish that, six of their members, including the four leaders of the fledgling church, set out for Guatemala. They had in mind no less a mission than experiencing the beauty and misery of a Third World country. They wanted to practice contemplation in a "poor" neighboring land —to see what the Lord would say to them. Representatives of Christian communities in Guatemala helped them plan their visit, and later became their guides, interpreters and pastors as they walked through the squalor and slums of a city, examined earthquake ruins, and talked with government leaders.

In the interior of the country where staff members of World Neighbors lived and worked they were able to see with their own eyes the difference that a small band of committed people had made in the life of one Indian village. Something happened deep in their beings as they talked with the people and were shown the new houses that the villagers had built with native material and—more especially—with their own hands. The Dunamis members began to yearn that others would have the same experience. "For it was *life* which appeared before us: we saw it, we are eye-witnesses of it..." (1 John 1:1–5 Phillips Modern English).

When the travellers were back home again, their energies flowed toward the development of a program that would make it easy for the thousands of Christians who travel each year to choose a journey purposely designed to expand the mind and heart, and to eliminate the divisions between the rich and poor. John Owens penned the travel folder for a vacation package that was to stand in contrast to the advertisements on "Bible Seminars in the Holy Land" and "Get Away" flights to exotic lands. The six-page leaflet included these statements:

1. Each year, for the next five years, an exploratory trip will be made to a different Third or Fourth World country.

2. Persons making these journeys outward, will do so as a part of Christ's Body and under the authority of the Holy Spirit. Disciplines of daily prayer, Scriptures, and journaling will be basic, as well as frequent worship together.

3. Help will be given for the inward journey of engagement with God and self, and for the outward journey of engagement with the poor of a third world country.

4. The hope is that every trip will generate one or more mission groups in the United States to nurture and develop third or fourth world linkages.

5. In the planning stage is the development of a framework for channeling money and other resources to the poor of the world.

While the travel program was being initiated several of the

Dunamis people took to Members of Congress material documenting the stories of Guatemalan farmers who had been reduced to extreme poverty because relief food shipments from the United States had driven the prices of food so low that they were unable to sell their own produce. The country did not need the corn of well-meaning neighbors. They did need money to buy the corn wasting in the bins of their own farmers.

Members of Congress began an investigation and the young church took fresh heart. A new spirit grew up in the small group. Though the members and intern members can be seated around one large table, they give the impression of being hundreds in number. Their movement is full of grace and confidence, and they talk about this project and that project as though it is only a matter of time before they are all accomplished. One can understand why the Egyptians were fearful of a band of slaves who had begun to realize that the power did not rest with Pharoah but within themselves. The members of the young church are also in on the secret of their own power. They, too, have discovered that they are free to break out of bondage, sing songs, laugh and create a new civilization.

The travellers had looked upon some of the agony of a land, had touched the garments of healers along the way and had, themselves, become healers. In the community everyone is exercising imagination and beginning to have visions and to hear God's summoning voice. In the other new communities we sometimes grumbled that we had too much to do, or too few people who share our thoughts. The Dunamis people seem unaware that they might be spreading themselves thin, or might lack the help they need.

One member announced that she would work in prisons and promptly began visiting prisoners. The oldest member—three score years and ten—called into being the Other Americans Mission Group, committed to working with Latinos in the area and to raising the consciousness of North Americans to the presence of South Americans. Others are giving their attention to "job conversion" or "job creation," so that gifts and ministries can be exercised under the authority of God rather than under the authority of institutions that are centered on profits rather than on people.

As for the travellers, they are making preparation to travel again. This time to India. They will take others with them, and stand beside them while they draw close to the misery of human beings and ask the question we all will ask who touch in any genuine way the suffering of the poor: "What must I do to be saved and to save?"

As the Dunamis Vocations Church, Wellspring, and other mission groups in the young churches deal in fresh ways with the issues raised around the theme of money, the subject has been introduced into the educational programs of the new communities. Some of us are angry to have so private a subject be given so public an airing. We would like to keep our economics and faith two separate spheres, and not be asked to consider that there might be some mysterious link between them. In the churches where we were raised there had been no connection between Jesus Christ and caring for the poor. We state again that "we are saved by faith and not by works."

Others of us are relieved to have a place in which we can explore more thoroughly the nagging issues around our money. We are feeling a kind of joy—you might say wild excitement—as though the raising of the whole subject is the prelude to a drama in which we shall cast our bread upon the water and join God's liberation movement on behalf of the earth's poor.

Still others harbor the fear that we will never "let go," and are all the more troubled because we wonder at the fate of those who know what we know, and still "hang on." We have reread the story of a rich man and a poor man who died, and the words of a father have a freshness in our hearts:

"Remember, my child, that all the good things fell to you while you were alive, and all the bad to Lazarus: now he has his consolation here and it is you who are in agony. But that is not all: there is a great chasm fixed between us; no one from one side who wants to reach you can cross it, and none may pass from your side to us" (Luke 16:25–27 NEB).

We wonder if anyone will ever sing for us:

> God rest you merry, Gentlemen,
> (God rest you merry, Ladies)
> Let nothing you dismay,
> Remember Christ our Saviour
> was born on Christmas day;

We all yearn to know again that Christ is born in us, for as St. Augustine said, ". . .this birth is always happening, but if it happens not in me what does it profit me? What matters is that it shall happen in me."

*Elizabeth*

P.S. The following assignment given in one of our classes might be helpful to you as you consider the dangerous subject of your money:

## ASSIGNMENT

Read Luke 12.

Write a three-page autobiography which deals with the meaning of money in your life. These are questions you might want to address in your account:

What is your happiest memory in connection with money? What is your unhappiest memory?

What role did money have in your childhood? What attitude did your mother have toward money? What attitude did your father have? What was your attitude toward money as a child? Did you feel poor? Or rich? Did you worry about money?

What was your attitude toward money as a teenager? What are your memories of this period?

What role did money play in your life as a young adult? As a parent? At age forty-seven? fifty-four? sixty-one? sixty-eight?. . . Did your attitude or feelings shift at different stages in your life?

What is your present financial status? How do you feel about it? What is your monthly income? What are your other assets? What will your income be at age sixty-five? seventy-five? eighty? Will you inherit money? Do you think about that? What do you consider responsible planning for the future? What is hoarding? At what point is security a valid issue? At what point is it invalid?

Are you generous or stingy with your money? Do you spend money on yourself? If so, do you do it easily? Do you feel guilty about the money you have? Do you feel grateful? Do you count your money? Do you take risks with your money? Do you gamble with your money? How? Do you "throw it away"? How? Do you worry about money? Do you have feelings of anger or resentment about money? When? Be specific.

When you dine out with friends and there is a single check, are you the one to pick it up? Or do you make sure that you pay your share, including the tax and tip? If not, what do you think this might tell you about yourself?

Do you tend to be more on the giving end of things, or on the receiving end? How does this make you feel?

If you lacked money, how would you feel about having others help pay your rent, or treat when you were not in a position to reciprocate?

If you had money, how would you feel about subsidizing a friend's rent, or paying more than your share of things? What would you want in return? How would you feel if that friend then spent money on something that in your value system was "extravagant"?

Can the poor and the rich live happily together? If your answer is "yes," what do you think it requires of each? If your answer is "no," why did you come to this conclusion?

Is it possible to value an independent life, and not fear dependency?

What is your response to Eliot's words:

> "Father, nobody can work with the poor and not fall over Karl Marx from time to time—or just fall over the Bible, as far as that goes. I think it's terrible the way people don't share things in this country. I think it's a heartless government that will let one baby be born owning a big piece of the country, the way I was born, and let another baby be born without owning anything. The least a government could do, it seems to me, is to divide things up fairly among the babies. Life is hard enough, without people having to worry themselves sick about money, too. There's plenty for everybody in this country, if we'll only share more."

Do you tithe or give away a proportion of your money? If so, how do you really feel about it? Do you tithe because this is how you want your money used, or do you tithe because you want to belong and are willing to pay this cost of belonging? Do you feel the money you are giving away is being used to build a more just and caring society? Do you feel these are guilt-producing questions? If your answer is yes, why?

## NOTES

1. Wellspring is a Mission of The Church of the Saviour to build and nurture faith communities. In addition to workshops on such subjects as money, anger, and peacemaking, the mission gives weekend seminars and eight-day workshops for ministers and lay leaders struggling for a deeper understanding of what it means to be the church in today's world.
2. *The Complete Short Stories of D. H. Lawrence* (New York: The Viking Press, Inc., 1971), pp. 790–791.
3. (New York: Dell Publishing Co., Inc., 1965), pp. 89–90.
4. A small Christian community committed to a life together, a ministry in the inner city, and an outreach that includes the publication of the *Sojourners* magazine.
5. "The Prisoner of Chillon."
6. Conscientization is the English translation for conscientizacao, a Spanish word that has grown up in the vocabularies of liberation theology. Paulo Friere writes that it refers to "learning to perceive social, political, and economic contradictions, and to take action against the oppressive elements of reality." *Pedagogy of The Oppressed* (New York: Herder and Herder, 1972), p. 19.

# 4

# *ON* KEEPING A JOURNAL

*Dear Sisters and Brothers:*

A few months ago I had a letter from a clinical psychologist who was with our church several years ago. It began:

> Help! I'm in need of guidance/resources/references in keeping a journal. About five years ago I regularly kept a journal; now I just can't keep with it. The problem in part is that I frequently ask others to keep a journal and hold them accountable for this discipline. I have found the journal extremely helpful in counseling with people of all ages and in consulting with other professionals seeking insight and new direction. Yet I can't hold to it in my own life.

I want to respond to the request by a letter to the scattered church, because I believe many of us can identify with that cry for help. In our small groups we know what it is to struggle with the discipline of keeping a journal. Like every other discipline, this one is easy for some and difficult for others. Also, as the above letter makes clear, what is easy at one stage is difficult at another, a fact that ought to keep us all humble.

It is a comforting reality that there is not a right or wrong way to keep a journal. If we will, ourselves, become readers of journals—aware of the different types—we will be helped in the keeping of our own. We can draw on one form or another to suit our needs, as we do in prayer. We cannot use the contemplative way of prayer when we want to cry for mercy or rage against our enemies. Writing in our journals seems to me to be very close to praying, if indeed it is not prayer. We cannot write our spiritual insights about the world when we have ourselves "on our hands." Our inner condition may be a helpful guide in our choice of a form of journal writing for a given day or period in our life.

Some journal keepers have recorded only the external scene —the people they met, places they went, things they saw and did. Many travelers keep this kind of journal so that they can look back and recall what otherwise might be lost to memory. In his own journal Thoreau wrote, "Wherever men have lived there is a story to be told. . . . You are simply a witness on the stand to tell what you know about your neighbors and neighborhood."

Others are more intrigued by the unseen, invisible world, and communion with that world. The outstanding representative of this kind of journalist is Dag Hammarskjöld. As Secretary General of the United Nations he moved among the leaders of the world and dealt with the crucial issues of governments, but in his journal, *Markings,* no names are noted nor any outward events described. He records not encounters with statesmen or travels back and forth across oceans, but his meeting with another order—the reality of another claim upon him.

Other journalists have not been able to write of the spiritual without grounding it in the whole created order, including very ordinary events. The journals of the Quakers, John Woolman and George Fox combine very naturally both emphases.

Another kind of journal, one which has become more popular in our day, honestly records emotional experiences, feelings and motivations. In this category we might place *The Confessions of St. Augustine* and Rousseau's *Confessions.* Interestingly enough, both books have "confession" in the title. Actually, any journal which attempts to deal honestly with the writer's feelings will have the confessional note simply because our feelings are always ambiguous, and if we are truthful about them our shadow self will show.

Still another type of journal which merits the special consideration of serious pilgrims is concerned primarily with self-discovery. This is the form of journal-keeping that I want to explore with you. Sometimes it has been called a psychological journal, but I resist that designation because of the many Christians who still feel that the psychological cannot also be spiritual. This kind of journal-keeping more than any other has the possibility of leading us on to the holy ground of our own lives. For easy reference I shall call this type the pilgrim journal. Though it includes the element of confession—self-disclosure —the form is for the writer primarily concerned with new understandings about self. In this respect it differs from Rousseau's *Confessions*, a fact on which Karen Horney, the psychoanalyst, commented:

> . . . Here is a man who apparently wants to give an honest picture of himself, and does so to a moderate extent. But throughout the book he retains blind spots concerning his vanity and his inability to love—to mention only two outstanding factors—which are so blatant that they impress us today as grotesque. He is frank about what he expects and accepts from others, but he interprets the resulting dependency as "love." He recognizes his vulnerability but relates it to his "feeling heart." He recognizes his animosities, but they always turn out to be warranted. He sees his failures, but always others are responsible for them.[1]

I cringe a little when I read that commentary on Rousseau. Part of me wonders if I, too, mistake my dependency for love. When I am hurt I explain it in terms of a sensitive nature. My anger is always a normal response to situations of injustice. As for my failures, I cannot look very long within myself for the answer to them. I move quickly to the "but. . ." that will place them firmly out there. "The fault, dear Brutus, is not in ourselves, but in our stars. . . ." I also know that it is one thing to give intellectual assent to the theory that I have blind spots, and another to believe it at an emotional level.

Reading the journals of others will increase our awareness of the choices we have in the writing of our own. My journal combines all forms. Before saying any more about the pilgrim journal, let me make a few elementary suggestions that I think will be helpful.

First, buy a good loose-leaf journal. An investment in a good journal indicates a seriousness of purpose, and will reinforce your belief that a record of your life is worth cherishing. If it is loose-leaf, you can remove a portion of it that you would like to share. Always date the pages so that they can be easily returned to place, as well as provide you with a time reference.

Second, always write your journal for yourself. Though it is true that you may want to share it, never write it with this in mind. Once you begin to entertain that thought in your writing, your internal censorship bureau—you have one—will spring into action to prevent a lot of important information and expression of feeling from emerging. Like censorship bureaus everywhere it will try to prevent you and others from coming into possession of secret files, full of hidden ambitions, claims, hopes and fears—all the data you need for the overthrow of oppressive systems in your life.

All of this may raise the question, how does one keep a journal private? John Wesley, the founder of Methodism, wrote his most private journals in a code of his own devising. He used three different systems of shorthand, letters, symbols, dots and dashes. For 250 years no one has been able to trace the key. Recently it was discovered by Richard Heitzenrater, a young American scholar, who has been granted permission to make a full transcription of ten small leather-bound diaries. A news story from the Manchester Guardian, England, states that they will be completed within the next two years and published by 1982 as part of a major work on Wesley. "What are the diaries expected to reveal? Heitzenrater would only say yesterday: 'The diaries show a tremendous amount about his personal thoughts and relationships.' "[2]

Now we will be able to look more deeply into the heart of a great leader, perhaps know some of the things that troubled him. We may even gain a few insights. What most of us need more to know, however, is that the world is trustworthy, that promises will be kept, and that we can choose with whom to share our secrets. In a technological world where privacy is invaded on every hand we yearn in vain for that demonstration of respect for another's wishes. In the meantime publishing houses continue to issue the private letters and journals of anyone who might have an audience.

A number of persons in my community have willed their journals to trusted persons who have promised to destroy them without reading them. Usually, however, our fears are more related to the present. We are afraid that the members of our own household will find our journals and read them. They do not have to be full of dark secrets for us to want to keep them private. Journals are an extension of ourselves. They say something about what is going on in the inner rooms of our lives. To pick up another's journal and to read it are like entering a person's house without an invitation and ransacking it—searching here and there for what one might find valuable. In the psychic life it is the equivalent of forced entry or rape. If we are fearful that the people in our households might read our journals, it would be helpful to take the risk of discussing our fears with them. A person might encroach on another's privacy by reading his journal because he is not conscious of the significance of what he is doing, or of the effect it will have on the writer. Every one of us has huge gaps in our education, and must endeavor to be in the world a gentle, caring and forgiving educator.

As for ourselves, let us never go unbidden over the threshold of another's life. If we want to know what is happening with another person, there are better ways of finding out. The best might simply be to ask. If that doesn't work, there may be other questions to ask of ourselves. We could have before us a larger task than we guessed—the one of making ourselves into the kind of persons with whom others want to share themselves.

Having said the foregoing, let me add that we are all attracted by the forbidden and given to impulses that we regret. We do not leave our money lying around when we know that it might tempt someone. The same cautions apply to journals. They should not be left lying round lest they tempt that good and natural curiosity that we have about each other.

Third, the keeping of a pilgrim journal requires a conscious, unswerving commitment to honesty with one's self . . . the first requirement for growth in self-understanding. No one can break our chains for us. We have to do this for ourselves. We may have some help along the way, but we are the only ones that

can set ourselves free, and this we do by coming into possession of truth—by routing out lies and deceits. This takes a lot
of courage, a lot of endurance, a commitment to press on when
we want to shrink back. <u>The goal is to make Jesus Christ the
Lord of our life.</u>

Surely for this kind of journey these scriptures from Ephesians were written:

> Finally then, find your strength in the Lord, in his mighty power.
> Put on all the armour which God provides, so that you may be able
> to stand firm against the devices of the devil. For our fight is not
> against human foes, but against cosmic powers, against the authori-
> ties and potentates of this dark world, against the superhuman
> forces of evil in the heavens. Therefore, take up God's armour; then
> you will be able to stand your ground when things are at their worst,
> to complete every task and still to stand. Stand firm, I say. Fasten
> on the belt of truth; for coat of mail put on integrity; let the shoes
> of your feet be the gospel of peace, to give you firm footing; and
> with all these, take up the great shield of faith, with which you will
> be able to quench all the flaming arrows of the evil one. Take
> salvation for helmet; for sword, take that which the Spirit gives
> you—the words that come from God. Give yourselves wholly to
> prayer and entreaty; pray on every occasion in the power of the
> Spirit. To this end keep watch and persevere.
>
> (Eph. 6:10–18 NEB)

No less than this kind of armour is needed for the person who
wants to work through to a place of liberation in her life. Anyone who embarks on an inward journey with any earnestness
knows that he is up against dark immemorial forces—principalities of evil entrenched in the inner sanctuaries of our own
beings. No decisive victory will go to the fainthearted or be
easily won.

One way to begin writing a journal is to give yourself to
prayer in the way of the psalmists who knew that they were
entitled to all of their feelings. They had faith that the God who
gave them such a rich and varied range of emotions was a God
who could hear cries of anguish and revenge as well as litanies
of gratitude and praise.

The prayers in which you do not hold back yourself will

become in time your own collection of psalms. In their first writing, however, do not give attention to literary composition. Another place and time may be appropriate for that. In your journal simply put down all your thoughts and feelings whether they move violently or stir ever so faintly in you. God and his world both want a relationship with you, and neither of those relationships can exist apart from the revelation of yourself. Out of the ensuing dialogue comes self-knowledge, which is essential for spirituality.

To work consistently on an exercise in self-observation is another important practice. A helpful place to start is to detect ourselves lying. Lying always separates us from ourselves. But we are not only capable of lying; we all do lie. Of course, the reason that might be a startling statement is that we lie to ourselves. This is what makes lying to others so dangerous. We actually come to believe the things that we say and the things that we write. We start out by trying to keep the truth from others and we end up by keeping the truth from ourselves.

The writer Maurice Nicoll says that the worst form of lying is pretense. "Everyone," he writes, "pretends to be what he is not. . . .We form in ourselves a kind of secret imagination and although life itself does not correspond to this secret imagination we still cling to it, feeling we are lions, eagles, supermen, etc., and never realize what we actually are like."[3] He suggests that we all harbor the feeling that we are able to speak the unbiased truth about ourselves and others, but that in actuality we are more apt to tell something in such a way that we are reflected in a favorable light. At least all of our sins are not revealed. We do this by leaving some facts out or overemphasizing others. Of course, the opposite is always possible. We may make things worse than they are, or put ourselves down so that we can gain sympathy or understanding or help. He explained:

> A person can lie with a single gesture, a single look, a single intonation, a casual mannerism, a sigh, a heartbroken expression, an illness, by a hearty manner, by being always fit and well. . . .When we are based on this inner self-romance we are very weak, whether the self-romance is about being strong and cheerful, or being misunderstood, or never having had a chance, etc. . . .It prevents us

[from] seeing our lives as they are, and asking ourselves this rather terrible question—why has your life been like this?[4]

The Potter's House worship bulletin has this confession:

We have been called to freedom, but we have found the burden heavy, the anxiety painful and have returned to our illusions about life and our deceits about ourselves.

Jeremiah put it very bluntly:

The heart is the most deceitful of all things, desperately sick; who can fathom it? (Jer. 17:9 NEB)

The New Testament addresses the matter directly:

Stop lying to one another, now that you have discarded the old nature with its deeds and have put on the new nature...."
(Col. 3:9–10 NEB)

I am suggesting that we include in our pilgrim journals an exercise to observe lying in ourselves. To the extent we can fasten on the belt of truth, to that extent will we be able to come into possession of new inner terrain. Each day record in your journal your observations about pretense and insincerity in yourself. Write about these things as fully as possible, and then ask yourself, "What have I skipped?" You will find yourself discovering things you missed.

The writing will increase your consciousness of intellectual and emotional dishonesty or insincerity within yourself. You will find yourself struggling oftener with the temptation to pretend. Consider what it was that you were trying to gain for yourself. What was the impression you were trying to give? What image were you trying to protect? Were you passing off borrowed opinions and thoughts as your own? What are your own wishes, desires, thoughts, feelings? Do not assume that you know.

Among our primary tools for growth are *reflection, self-observation* and *self-questioning*. The journal is one of the most helpful vehicles we have for cultivating these great powers in ourselves. We all have these powers but we need structures that encourage us to use and practice them. Journal writing is enforced reflection. When we commit our observations to writing we are taking what is inside us and placing it outside us. We are holding a piece of our life in our hands where we can look at it, and meditate on it, and deepen our understanding of it.

Beginning our work of observation by discerning our tendency to lie develops our capacity for openness and honesty, puts us in touch with our real self, and helps that self to make the movement toward becoming God's word in the world.

While the recognition of our lying self comprises an important area for self-study, it is best to be guided by what pulls at one's own heart when choosing an exercise in observation. If you are troubled because you have begun to feel that you are by nature too critical, this might be the important area to explore. Begin by noting all the times that you are critical, what provokes criticism in you, and how you express it. Notes taken over several months may indicate that it matters little what the occasion is or who is involved—you react the same way and say pretty much the same things. Look for the opposite in yourself —in this case, praise and confirmation. If you cannot find it, it is because its expression has been too long blocked.

Another fruitful field for study is the area of our complaints. It is very easy to become a chronic complainer—never to face the source of our discontent, never to address the crucial question of what we might do to set things right for ourselves.

Design your own exercise, and glean what you can from the practice of it. Write your thoughts down as they come to you, giving them free reign. This is the way to forge new paths for the release of spirit in yourself. Later comes the work of questioning. To be sure we lose touch with our feelings and do not know the intensity of our anger or our hate, but even to know these feelings and to find a nonviolent outlet for them are not sufficient. Our problems do not go away so quickly. Screaming out our anger may be better than having it erupt in painful joints, migraine headaches, or ulcerated stomachs, but the relief is not that lasting, nor are the problems of our living that easily settled. Pounding on pillows will help us to take the first step of knowing the intensity of our anger, but it is only a first step.

Karen Horney gives hints of the work to be done. She maintains that it is easier to be angry than to look within for the vulnerable spot that has been hit. It really doesn't matter how cruel, unfair or inconsiderate the other has been, we are not let off the hook. She illustrates this by an example of hurt that might be justified:

> Let us assume that a wife is deeply disturbed at learning that her husband has had a transient affair with another woman. Even months later she cannot get over it, although she knows it is a matter of the past and although the husband does everything to re-establish a good relationship. She makes herself and him miserable, and now and then goes on a spree of bitter reproaches against him. There are a number of reasons that might explain why she feels and acts in this way, quite apart from a genuine hurt about the breach of confidence. It may have hurt her pride that the husband could slip out from her control and domination. The incident may have touched off a dread of desertion. She may be discontented with the marriage for reasons of which she is not aware, and she may use this conspicuous occurrence as an excuse for expressing all her repressed grievances, thus engaging merely in an unconscious campaign of revenge. She may have felt attracted toward another man and resent the fact that her husband indulged in a freedom that she had not allowed herself. If she examined such possibilities she might not only improve the situation considerably but also gain a much clearer knowledge of herself. Neither result is possible, however, as long as she merely insists upon her right to be angry. The situation would be essentially the same if she had repressed her anger, though in that case it would be much more difficult to detect her resistance toward self-examination.[5]

Self-justification is one of the first things we must give up if we are to know the real reason of our grief. The Book of Wisdom cautions that those who do not know the cause of their suffering will remain locked in sleep, subject to having unexpected fears sweep over them, as well as being "chased by monstrous spectres." To be sure there is darkness over us, but heavier than the darkness is the burden we can be to ourselves. (Wisdom, Chapter 17)

Sometimes your thoughts will take you down false trails; other times they will go some place. You do not have to find God at the end of every path. As myth and legend tell us it is often where we falter and stumble that we find the treasure. After several months or several years of "journaling," as we refer to it in our communities, when you read what you have written you will be able to see themes and characteristic responses that you were not aware of in the writing. The "dead ends" may have important things to say to you.

If your small group or community has the discipline of keeping a journal, or you have agreed with another person to keep this discipline, you may want to decide together on an exercise in self-observation. When you meet you will be helped if you will share jottings from your journal.

In the letter I quoted at the beginning you will note that the writer complains that, though he asks others to keep a journal and holds them accountable for the discipline, he cannot hold to it in his own life. My guess is that he, himself, has no one who holds him accountable. If someone is asking us to give account we receive encouragement and support for overcoming obstacles in ourselves. In my own mission group, we give to the spiritual director each week a written report on how we succeeded or failed in keeping this and other disciplines. In our reports which, unlike our journal writing, we write specifically for another's eyes, we include observations and findings that we feel good about sharing with another. Having a loose-leaf journal makes it possible to include these weekly sheets of accountability as part of one's journal.

Last week when my mission group met I did not have my report, and my spiritual director asked whether I would give it to him in the morning. When I hestitated a bit, he said he would come by and pick it up. My spiritual director happens to live in the basement apartment of my building, a very fine arrangement for one planning to be serious in this matter of keeping a journal. Most of you, however, will not be so fortunate as to have your spiritual director living in your basement. The best that I can hope for you is that your guide or "faithful friend" will be firm and hold you responsible for that which you said you wanted to do.

The question of accountability raises the whole issue of resistance, which is the enemy of our freedom and must be overcome. If we do suspend, as best we can, our tendency to censor and allow ourselves freely to commit our feelings and thoughts to paper, things we did not guess were there will begin to surface. We might, for example, discover that we have some very negative feelings about a person toward whom we thought we felt all loving and warm. We may even begin to wonder whether this might account for the vague feeling of anxiety that we always have when in this person's company. If we are on a path toward the discernment of material that has been hidden from us, we are apt to meet with counter-revolutionary forces in our household. We might find ourselves too tired to write in our journals, not as interested as we thought we were, or despairing of the good such an effort will do us.

Despite the necessity of a commitment to honesty, it can apply only to that known area of ourselves, or to those areas of pretense that lie close to the surface of consciousness. The fact is, however, a lot of what we believe to be truth may not be truth. We may be acting in a very modest, unassuming way when actually we have a driving ambition to get ahead and to come out first. We may do everything to protect an image of ourselves as giving and generous, when in fact we have a great need to hang on to what we have.

This conflict often results in the fear of being found out, a fairly common fear. Of course, you might ask, "How can anyone have that fear who is not even aware of pretending?" The fact is that, by God's grace, though we succeed to a large extent in fooling ourselves, we never fully succeed. Deep down a part of us knows the truth—a truth which makes itself known in our dreams, in the comparisons we make, or in a disturbance that is evidenced in such an attitude as withdrawal.

Often the fear of being found out is diffused and may be experienced as a fear of, or a turning away from, intimacy. "If they come to know me, they will not like me—fail to find me as attractive or as intelligent as they thought." We all know that intimacy draws forth the worst in us as well as the best. Whatever our illusions or deceits about ourselves may be, defences are built to protect us from recognizing them. We need to feel safe and secure. We have a compelling interest in blinding ourselves to anything that does not fit in with our image of who we are. If we want some idea of why the structures of society are resistant to change, we have only to study ourselves.

No part of the unconscious is going to be handed over to the conscious without a big battle. The forces against liberation are known as "resistance." Part of us knows that if we want to be free something radical has to happen. We have to change a part of the foundation of our house. How many of us have had the help and insight we needed to build on rock? The floods and the winds come—people do not respond as we think they should. They fail to come when we call to them, or to go where we tell them to go, or to understand what we are trying to communicate. More than that, they, too, live in houses that are not on rock.

A pilgrim journal is a way to still the waters and hold back the winds—to discern where the forces of liberation clash with the forces of oppression. We may make the discovery that we need the help of a faithful friend, a spiritual director, a group, or a therapist who can give emotional support, encouragement and supplies to the embattled forces of our own revolutionary army.

The subject of "resistance" is one that Karen Horney develops in her book, *Self-Analysis.* We will find no better guide or help in keeping a journal than this book, which includes an account of the author's work with patients who kept journals of self-discovery. Her writing transmits her faith in the capacity of persons to get in touch with the unknown in themselves. She gives instruction in the art of free association, a practice which deserves an important place in journal writing. One simply writes whatever happens to come to mind—thoughts, images, dreams, fantasies, feelings, sensations. Thinking spontaneously—letting the thoughts and images flow—requires practice. One becomes an observer of what flashes across the screen of the mind, jotting down only the word or two necessary to recall it, freely attending to the next image, thought, or feeling.

As in psychoanalysis, the journalist gives his or her thoughts free expression. Dr. Horney gives us this wisdom:

> . . .There is no doubt whatever that whether one is working alone or with an analyst the greatest obstacles to free expression are always within oneself. One is so anxious to ignore certain factors and to maintain one's image of oneself, that alone or not alone one

can hope only to approximate the ideal of free associations. In view of these difficulties the person who is working alone should remind himself from time to time that he acts against his true self-interest if he skips or obliterates any thought or feeling that arises. Also, he should remember that the responsibility is entirely his own; there is no one but himself to guess a missing link or inquire about a gap left open.

This conscientiousness is particularly important in regard to the expression of feelings. Here there are two precepts that should be remembered. One is that the person should try to express what he really feels and not what he is supposed to feel according to tradition or his own standards. He should at least be aware that there may be a wide and significant chasm between genuine feelings and feelings artificially adopted, and should sometimes ask himself— not while associating but afterward—what he really feels about the matter. The other rule is that he should give as free range to his feelings as he possibly can. This, too, is more easily said than done. It may appear ridiculous to feel deeply hurt at a seemingly trivial offense. It may be bewildering and distasteful to mistrust or hate somebody he is close to. He may be willing to admit a ripple of irritation, but find it frightening to let himself feel the rage that is actually there.[6]

Our dreams, of course, also have the possibility of putting us in touch with repressed feelings. One way of discovering the message is by attending to them. Keep your journal by your bed, so on waking you can write out your dream. Record the dream and then what comes to mind in connection with each part of it. Treat it as a stranger from a distant land bearing important information about your life. Carry your dream around with you until you have learned its language. Carry your journal around with you too. We shall profit greatly by becoming journal-toting pilgrims.

In deciding what to write about choose what strikes a deep chord in yourself. I call my own notebooks "dark journals," because I have strong motivation to write about what is troubling to me—feelings that I wish I did not have, resentments I cling to, relationships that cause me too much unhappiness, direction I cannot find and fears I cannot shake. For me one of the clear, ever present signs of God's moving in the world is that he has so fashioned us that we hurt when we are not thriving, giving, loving creatures. We know the pain of not growing when things go awry for us and we are not developing our potential. Anger and frustration both tell us that we have work to do. If we will settle down with these two emotions we will discover how painful they are. We may also discover how to heal ourselves.

God has so wondrously made us that we are capable of being aware of even a speck in the eye or a sliver in the finger. In our psychic life also our pain pleads for our attention. We are designed for unfolding in God's love. What would become of us if we had no disturbed feelings to let us know when we wander off the path of our salvation? Suppose we could do wrong and have no response of guilt, or that we could treat others with indifference without their knowing it or our knowing it. Of course, we can shut out our pain—harden our hearts—but it is quite obvious that God does not want his creatures to settle for less than the fullness of creation.

So what if we have obstacles to overcome in gaining self-knowledge? Again, how would our life be if everything were given to us and we did not have to work for it? True, we come up against large resistances, but what is so extraordinary about that? Every creator has that experience. Analysts write about the phenomenon of resistance in the field of self-discovery because that is the vineyard they know and in which they labor. Where is the artist who has not had to battle huge resistances to complete a work? I have heard in my life of a few compulsive writers who could not wait to get to the typewriter, but my friends do battle as I do with enormous forces in themselves before things begin to flow. The blocks are never overcome once and for all, which may mean that literature and art arise out of the unconscious, as perhaps does any creative work. Certainly the creation of one's life is a creative work, which is another way of describing what we are about in the keeping of a pilgrim journal.

Go with your feelings, choose the subject that captures your mind and heart. If you have never kept a journal you might begin by simply making lists of your loves, hates, desires, hopes. Write your journal against the backdrop of the questions: What do I feel? What do I choose? What do I want? What do I think?

Despite the promise of returns, I doubt that any of us will

invest ourselves in the keeping of a pilgrim journal, or be in any important way on the path of growth and transformation unless we have some very real intimation of how little we know ourselves. Freud said that what we see is only the tip of an iceberg. Each of us has a self that is largely unknown.

Very few religious people understand that self-knowledge is related to love. I keep repeating that thought because it is so poorly understood. When we wake up to truth in ourselves we wake up to the Divine in us. We discover our self-worth, our heritage, that we are sons and daughters of the Living God. He is the One who made us, who sent us into the world and will call us back to Himself.

In our journals we are in search of the real self—of what really moves us, what we really think, what we really feel. We live in a culture that values conformity more than uniqueness. We also have been raised in homes where, for one reason or another, we did not receive the love and confirmation that we needed. We have thus grown up forsaking ourselves in an effort to gain the emotional warmth and approval that is essential to a sense of well-being. Another of Freud's extraordinary insights was that if we do not find a warm relationship with a parent who is either too overpowering, or too withdrawn, or simply on a different wavelength, we make up for that lack of closeness by incorporating the parent into our own being. We do this by adopting his or her opinions, values, ideas, way of doing things, so that we have the person that we so need. Of course, in the process we become separated from our real selves, which never have an opportunity to develop in their own uniqueness. We find our centers outside ourselves.

A pilgrim journal belongs to a person of faith who believes in an unknown world within and a God who can raise the dead, cause streams to flow, and singing to break forth. All the unacceptable elements, rejected parts of ourselves can be baptized in the name of the Father and the Son and the Holy Ghost. We can claim new territories in ourselves. ". . .make disciples of all the nations" (Matt. 28:19 Jer.). This is the divine commission. We do not have to worship God with just the tips of ourselves or view his world with planks in our eyes.

Whoever joins God's liberation movement must be content

to spend time in the wilderness, to live in tents and not know what the morrow brings. We seek God's will so that we can let our lives unfold according to his design. We look "forward to a city founded, designed and built by God" (Heb. 11:10 Jer.). To the extent that we have been able to be our own persons— subject and obedient to the one true God—to that extent we are persons on pilgrimage. Do not believe, however, that we will never listen to other voices, never lose our way or follow the path of least resistance—which means settling for things as they are—dwelling in flat country where the wind does not blow.

I can hear some of you saying, "But the way of self-discovery seems like so self-centered a way. Our goal should be to forget self and focus on God and his work" as though we were not God's work. I have lost the patience I once had for those who raise this objection to self-study. I am beginning to think that in the name of God these folk deter too many people from understanding an important pilgrimage.

When we discourage persons from being on an inward journey of self-discovery, we keep them from coming into possession of their own souls, keep them from finding the eternal city, keep them from being authentic persons who use their gifts and personality to mediate God's peace and God's love. He or she who tries to keep another from the pilgrim path of self-discovery is doing the devil's work, and a lot of frightened persons are about that work. Of course, the resistances that these folk have to looking at themselves is not any different from the resistances the rest of us have. The difference lies in their use of religious words and distorted religious teachings to make themselves feel secure in their position. They even go so far as to imply that those of us committed to this inward journey are less Christian, less committed, less capable of caring for others. They label us "humanistic" or "too psychologically oriented," as though God cared neither for humans nor for psychologists. As a result many of God's flock go about looking at his world through clouded lenses, using church projects to build up wobbly self-esteem, enlisting dependent people to foster their phony selves, passing off a neurotic need for affection as a loving, caring nature, or the compulsion to be ever busy as priestly concern. Such persons have within themselves all kinds of conflicts which produce dissension in the groups to which they belong. Their vulnerability, excessive demands, expectations and criticisms make genuine community almost impossible.

In some degree such a description applies to each one of us and, although ours may be different from that of our neighbor, we are nonetheless in the grip of some sort of neurotic trend. As a young student I was once in a lecture hall where Karen Horney was asked the question, "Have you ever known anyone who was not neurotic?" She answered, "No, I never have, though perhaps in some remote, uncontaminated part of the world it might be possible that someone could grow up free of neuroses." This is not to say that we are all equally in the grasp of the devil. Some of us are healthier and freer than others, but to everyone is given the instruction, "Take the beam out of your own eye" and, above all, do not prevent your brothers and sisters from entering into their heritage. Of you to whom much has been given, much will be required.

Let us not assume, however, that psychology and the pursuit of self-knowledge automatically lead to a God-committed life. The release of gifts and the development of potentials can be used to dominate others and to grab more of the world's goods. This movement out of one sick cycle into another is all the more alarming because the world shares the illusion that such persons are healthy, prospering and eminently successful. The Church bears some responsibility for this state of affairs. We have not modeled in a convincing way the joys and satisfactions of another way. We have not made it clear that one of the chief concerns of the Church is to help each person to realize his potential, to discover the work he is to do and to find a people with whom to cast his lot.

In ourselves are vast unknown areas. Once this discovery is made one begins to realize that his own life can never be completely known. Myself is the stranger. In a sense, the stranger is always the enemy who, if we will take the risk of knowing, may become friend. Then we will not have to run madly about in the space outside us, demanding community. If we can learn to seek out and keep company with the real self that is within, we will discover that this self is the most interesting self we can ever know—full of contradictions, deceits, wonders, gifts and untold possibilities. To know one's self is the largest task given to any one of us. Hearing that, even believing it, does not in any way approximate the experiencing of it.

To accept the fact that one's life is only partially known is to stand before it with the sense of awe and of mystery that the unknown always elicits. Then we are able to stand before every other life with a growing sense of reverence, wonder, awe and mystery. The acknowledgement of this unknown, mysterious territory in each of us is what makes relationship the most exciting of all adventures. Every time I meet with you there is the possibility that we will come to a deeper knowing of one another and a deeper knowing of ourselves. As I am in touch with my truth, I have the possibility of putting you in touch with your truth and as you touch truth in yourself you give to me that same possibility.

People fail to find each other interesting because the reality of the self as stranger and the other person as stranger is not in any marked degree accepted. Despite what we may say, we really do not have that much interest in knowing ourselves. That being true, we do not—cannot—have any genuine interest in knowing the other person, or in believing that there is something more to know about her than we already know. We may assent at one level to this business of getting to know ourselves, but at another level my guess is that not many people really feel that they are all that mysterious, or that they have all that much to learn, when, in fact, a lifetime is actually not long enough to know what there is to know about any one person. This is why marriage is a reasonable and sacred covenant, which makes it possible for two people to live together in a deepening and expanding way. Marriage becomes very unreasonable when there are no rungs on the ladder, no work to do together, no place to go, no evolutionary possibility.

The keeping of a pilgrim journal is an important handle for opening the doors to the inner rooms of one's own house, and for discovering what lies hidden there. The pages of a journal kept over the days and weeks and months will help us in our pursuit of truth—in making God our aim. Journaling is not for people of unfaith (in the unconscious) or those who want to keep the status quo in their own lives. It is for adventurers, for those who have a vision of another city, who hear the call given to Abraham to leave the old land and to set out for a new one. Along the way you will have to do battle with the principalities of evil. The devil himself will try to shake your confidence. He will try to make you think that you are not all that important—not really worth the effort. Dis-ease shakes our confidence in what we can do, in who we are and in who we can become. We begin to doubt that there is a plan for us and a place where we fit in. Carried to its extreme, doubt whispers that God is not there and that he does not tend our life, that he will not complete what he has begun.

To undertake claiming yourself for yourself, take Ephesians, especially the words, "Take salvation for helmet; for sword, take that which the Spirit gives you—the words that come from God. Give yourselves wholly to prayer and entreaty; pray on every occasion in the power of the Spirit. To this end keep watch and persevere" (6:17–18 NEB).

If you are tempted to settle down, to call the journey off, nail these words over the door of your house, "If they had been thinking of that land from which they had gone out, they would have had opportunity to return. But as it is, they desire a better country" (Heb. 11:15–16 RSV).

May the Lord, Our God, keep us all persons of faith. May he help us to build a society that calls us each to conquer inner territory.

*Elizabeth*

## NOTES

1. *Self Analysis* (New York: W. W. Norton & Company, Inc., 1942), p. 294.
2. "The Decoding of John Wesley's Private Diaries," *The Washington Post,* Sept. 3, 1977.
3. Maurice Nicoll, *Psychological Commentaries* (London: Vincent Stuart & John M. Watkins Ltd., 1964), p. 608.
4. Nicoll, *Psychological,* p. 610.
5. *Self Analysis,* pp. 283–284.
6. *Self Analysis,* pp. 248–249.

# 5

## *ON*
## THE JOURNAL
## AND GROUP LIFE

*Dear Brothers and Sisters:*

I once had a friend who was the minister of two churches. He found it to be a fine arrangement. Whenever he felt swamped by the difficulties of one parish, he would spend most of his time with the other parish. I am reminded of this friend when I am tempted to cast about for another group belonging that will offer me more understanding and companionship, as well as escape from the conflicts and pressures that are generated by any small community from time to time.

I know from experience, however, as well as from the warnings of the wise, that every group is in microcosm the whole world. If we can deal with the obstacles that block deep and caring relationships between and among our own group members we will be learning how to deal with every other relationship in our lives.

A group constellates feelings that belong to us but are not always in our awareness when we are alone or with selected individuals. As Freud discerned, the emotions and experiences that we repress in childhood later find an outlet and are transferred to vague and analogous figures in the here and now. Eleanor Bertine, another psychoanalyst, wrote:

Some people try to keep out of collective life because the reactions set up in them by its impact are too powerful, too painful, too destructive to their ego values. But this undue vulnerability exists because too much of them is unconscious, amorphous, and shapeless, and therefore projected—for what is unconscious in us we always project. Whenever there is a flat place in the psychic development of a person, this unrealized content is apt to find someone in the group onto whom it will be projected. The projection brings the problem into visibility and is thereby the beginning of hell or redemption. . . .[1]

It is as though within the group we are given new chances to resolve old conflicts and to change what is a curse upon us into a blessing. A Hasidic teaching says:

God said to Abraham: "Get thee out of thy country, and from thy kindred, and from thy father's house, into the land that I will show thee." God says to man: "First, get you out of your country, that means the dimness you inflicted on yourself. Then out of your birthplace, that means out of the dimness your mother inflicted on you. After that, out of the house of your father, that means out of the dimness your father inflicted on you. Only then will you be able to go to the land that I will show you."[2]

When we do not face our hostilities, irritations, jealousies or envy, we become bogged down—lose our hope and sense of responsibility for the future. More than this the groups to which we belong suffer for whatever we fail to work through. They stumble along without power to effect change or mediate healing. Lives remain poor in relationship, and we hunger for community as though we were in no way accountable for its absence.

Small groups will always confront us with the problem of our projections, as well as with issues of authority, dependency, competition, intimacy and distance. We can avoid some of these encounters by avoiding group life. Many churches and individuals have chosen to do just this. To elect the way of withdrawal however may be to close the door on a storehouse of riches and perhaps to forego freedom itself. The "narrow way" mentioned in Scripture is to struggle for redemption—to cling in faith to humankind as it is represented by the members of our small communities. We cannot make it alone to the throne of God. Our destinies are forever interlocked.

What I am suggesting is that our membership in the Church

is going to give us mysteries in interpersonal relationships to work through, but that this can be gift—the road to a new land. We can reflect not only on those relationships in the present that trouble us, but on old relationships and the correspondence between the present and the past. The opportunity to examine the past should not be the privilege of the affluent few. Every adult ought to claim it, using his disturbed heart to stake his claim on virgin land where God's fresh breezes blow.

While counseling and therapy groups are convened to deal specifically with the problems that are activated and made visible among their members, they should not be given exclusive claim on this work. In his time with the twelve Christ worked with all the problems in interpersonal relationships that arise in any group that has a continuing life. What else could he do? He was preparing his little band to live together in such a way that people would know that they belonged to him by the way they were relating to each other. His disciples have that commission. If we are to build the church—a community of caring—each of us has the task of growing up into the mature stature of Christ, which means knowing something about what is in the hearts of all men and women, including not only the dark immemorial forces that can be unleashed by the collective, but the forces of light that can unite God's people into a liberation army.

I was recently in an all-day seminar for group therapy leaders who were working on the subject of resistance within groups. Someone asked the question, "What is the difference between a counseling group and a therapy group?" "One of the differences," said the leader, "is that the people in a therapy group are willing to say that they are patients."

I found this easy to understand. If one does not believe that in one's self are the blocks on the way to love and freedom, then what motivation would there be for self-questioning? In so unconscious a state one could not do the work essential for healing. "But why," I asked, "should this not be the requirement for counseling groups, since they also have healing in mind? And why should the task of educators not be to bring every person to an understanding of himself as the patient?"

Class members immediately resisted the definition of patient for themselves. They seemed to be saying that I was either too idealistic or too ignorant. Actually, I thought my understanding of patienthood was based on what depth psychologists had been saying about the ambiguities and fears that plague us all; but perhaps it was more rooted in my understanding of Scripture and of the nature of the church community. You come into church membership only by declaring yourself a sinner—in everyday talk, a patient. Is not this why the church can so confidently proclaim that each of us has the possibility of transformation?

The church is the people who take their patienthood with seriousness and give themselves to the work of their own healing, as well as to the healing of others. As in every other creative process this work requires a total commitment, but in the end its accomplishment is dependent on an act of grace. There is that part which we ourselves cannot do. Another Hasidic legend says:

> The souls descended from the realm of heaven to earth, on a long ladder. Then it was taken away. Now, up there, they are calling home the souls. Some do not budge from the spot, for how can they get to heaven without a ladder? Others leap and fall and leap again, and give up. But there are those who know well that they cannot achieve it, but try and try over and over again until God catches hold of them and pulls them up.[3]

Not only is so much of ourselves repressed or undiscovered, which is part of our patienthood, but our perception of what lies outside of us is distorted by our fears, illusions, self deceits, fantasies, experiences and prejudices. We do not see the world outside us any more accurately than we perceive the world within us.

There are some helping tools which can prove useful to us, both as we keep our pilgrim journals and as we share life with others in small groups. Let me share some of them.

In 1955 at the Western Training Lab in Group Development, Joe Luft and Harry Ingham used a diagram to help illustrate how things are with us. Since then it has been reproduced in a number of manuals for educators, and has become known as the Johari Window. The entire diagram is representative of the Self.

| OPEN | BLIND |
|---|---|
| (What is known to ourselves and known to others) | (What others know about us that we do not know about ourselves) |
| HIDDEN | UNKNOWN |
| (What we know about ourselves but choose not to reveal to others) | (The area of the unconscious, containing dung and treasure, loves and hates) |

Reflection is a way of altering our window. For example, if we begin to use our time of reflection and meditation to examine the area of ourselves that we keep private, we may discover that we do not share large parts of who we are. More than likely, this is because we ourselves want to avoid a closer look at them, or have undue shame or fear connected with them, rather than because of our usual declaration that everyone has a right to a private self, true though this be. As a result too many people are alone with their problems, putting up brave fronts for each other when they could be helping each other.

While some need to work with enlarging the open area of their window, others may want to increase the area of the private. We find ourselves blurting out what we would much prefer to hold closer to ourselves. As James knew so well, the tongue "is a small member but it can make huge claims" (James 3:5 NEB). He was distressed that praises and curses come out of the same mouth. Those of us who keep journals will be in better control of our tongues when we have written out some of the hurts and offenses we have suffered and when we have given expression to feelings of mistrust or revenge toward persons who are close to us, or with whom we would like to feel close. If we will use journals to explore the intensity of tender and hateful feelings, we will find ourselves becoming better communicators. Expressive and appropriate words will be available when the time of speech comes. The clearer we are about our feelings and desires, the better able we are to communicate them to others in a way they are able to understand.

The blind area in the Johari Window is the one that fills me with indignation. It seems unfair, even outrageous, that another should know things about me that I do not know about myself. The psalmist was more accepting when he wrote, "But who can detect his own feelings? Wash out my hidden faults" (Ps. 19:12 Jer.). If we can do battle with our pride and become sufficiently aware of our defenses to accept them and ourselves, we might fmd the motivation to ask others how they perceive us. Such a question requires a large degree of humility, the quality which God loves above all others in his creatures. "God, grant me humility," is a courageous prayer. In my experience he always rushes to answer it. I think of God as patiently waiting for us to make that prayer. Even though you only turn it over in your mind, he sends forth all his angels to arrange the circumstances of your enlightenment. Nonetheless, have no fear. If you have some emotional understanding of Freud's iceberg or the Johari Window you already have a degree of humility, which makes easier the process of acquiring more.

Those of you who have a small pilgrim group, or a companion with whom you are working, may decide that you want to share findings and questions from your journal. It may be a helpful practice to read selected portions of your journal aloud for someone else. Speech has a special power of its own. The utterance of our own words will put us in touch with new feelings and thoughts.

When we have finished reading, we might ask for feedback on some of our observations. "Have you noticed this about me?" "How do you perceive my response in that situation?"

The giving and receiving of helpful feedback is an extraordinary tool for self-discovery. Its use, however, requires special practice, but more than this, a large degree of sensitivity and an openness of heart. Most of us tend to discount even positive feedback. We are no more aware of our assets than of our liabilities. It is possible to be chronically angry because others do not hold us in the esteem that we know to be our due, and at the same time to think so poorly of ourselves that when others do mention our gifts or compliment us, we are embarrassed, brush their comments aside, or interrupt to move the conversation in another direction. Deep down we may think, "If she knew the truth about me, she would not be saying that." We do not take positive feedback home with us, write it in our journals, hold it in our hands and meditate on it. We do not give credence to the fact that others might see in us what we are unable to see in ourselves.

A low image of ourselves can prevent any serious consideration of the positive data that is all the time flowing into our lives. When we are locked into a poor self-image we also tend to disparage others, viewing them through a distorted lens. One way to work with this is to consciously seek to affirm others in the group—to give them positive feedback. No person is so poor that she does not have something to recommend her.

In a sermon on Jesus, Gerard Manley Hopkins wrote:

> But, brethren, from all that might be said of his character I single out one point and beg you to notice that. He loved to praise, he loved to reward. He knew what was in man, he best knew men's faults and yet he was the warmest in their praise. When he worked a miracle he would grace it with "Thy faith hath saved thee," that it might almost seem the receiver's work, not his. He said of Nathanael that he was an Israelite without guile; he that searches hearts said this, and yet what praise that was to give! He called the two sons of Zebedee Sons of Thunder, kind and stately and honourable name! We read of nothing thunderlike that they did except, what was sinful, to wish fire down from heaven on some sinners, but they deserved the name or he would not have given it, and he has given it them for all time. Of John the Baptist he said that his greater was not born of women. He said to Peter: Thou art Rock, and rewarded a moment's acknowledgment of him with the lasting headship of his Church. He defended Magdalen and took means that the story of her generosity  should be told for ever. And though he bids *us* say we are unprofitable servants, yet he himself will say to each of us: Good and faithful servant, well done.[4]

Feedback on our liabilities can be as revolutionary to our growth as feedback on our assets, but it is even more threatening to hear, especially when we have an inflated self-image, which is the other face of a poor self-image. Unless we have made some inward preparation we will find that we respond defensibly to any information that conflicts with an idealized picture of our self. We will tend to feel attacked and to counterattack.

I remember an evening as a child when my family was making the common observation that we all have faults of which we are unaware. We went on to agree that we would tell each other what we felt to be their liabilities. It seemed like a marvelous idea and we entered into the experience with a spontaneous and innocent joy, as though we were going to make life-changing discoveries about ourselves. Hurt and anger brought a quick end to the whole enterprise, and taught me the hazards of such an undertaking.

Most of us do not ask others for their feedback even when we take seriously the fact that they might know something about us that we do not know about ourselves. We are equally cautious about their feelings, and go to great lengths rather than tell them what they might not want to hear. We would rather walk away from a relationship than go through the pain of dealing with negative feelings.

Recently educators have seemed to be more optimistic about human nature, and have begun to give guidelines for effective feedback. Like every process that has potential for great good this one must be used in a responsible way. The following suggestions which appeared in a manual for adult learning,[5] might be helpful for anyone working with a group.

1. Feedback should not be *forced* or *imposed* on someone. When the receiver of feedback feels threatened, he does not learn, but tends to raise defenses and becomes closed. Mutual trust is needed for feedback to be received and to be effective.

2. Feedback is the perception of a person's *behavior,* and therefore, should not be presented as an attributed motive or actual intention of the person. Feedback is neither right nor wrong in itself, but rather the way the perceiver sees the situation. The perception of another's behavior needs to be confirmed by that person's own intentions and also checked out with other group members' perceptions.

3. Feedback should be clear, specific, and related to the "data," i.e., to actual incidents, examples, and observations of behavior. Judgments of a person's personality traits or vague generalizations are best avoided.

4. Feedback should be descriptive and potentially useful, while it should leave the receiver free to use or not use the information, as he sees fit.

Our reflection, self-questioning and self-observation help us to be in touch with feelings and thoughts of which we would otherwise be unaware in ourselves. We can then disclose some of these to others, who give us their feedback. As a result all four areas of the window are affected.

The following diagram illustrates the change that may take place:

THE JOHARI WINDOW

|  | Known to Self | Not known to Self |
|---|---|---|
| Known to Others | 1.<br>Area of Free Activity (Public Self) | 2.<br>Blind Area |
| Not Known to Others | 3.<br>Avoided or Hidden Area (Private Self) | 4.<br>Area of Unknown Activity |

Under conditions of self-disclosure

Under conditions of feedback

Under conditions of self-disclosure and feedback

The subject of feedback relates to journal keeping as well as to other areas of a pilgrim's life. Many of us are struggling with the keeping of a journal as a group discipline, but usually we are not realizing the advantages of working with a group. If a group uses journaling to work on its own life, all kinds of things can happen. Journaling on a subject that we plan to present to others prepares us for the hearing of another's response. To further help us in our listening we can also adopt the practice of not responding immediately, but jotting down notes on what persons say and using them later as material for meditation. We can then return to the group and share our reflections on what we thought we heard them saying, and how it affected us, always bearing in mind that we do not have to accept a group opinion as truth even if it is held by all the members. We can accept only what rings true in our own being.

By dying to false images and resolving conflicts and old grudges, we are freeing our energies to develop our potentials, to listen to call, and to get on with the whole matter of our vocation. We will then be moved to reflect upon our gifts. One of my favorite journal exercises for small groups is to have each member make a list of what he believes to be his gifts, and a similar list for other members in the group. Members then add to their lists the gifts listed by others. After that each person reads his list aloud. "What do you see as my gifts?" and "What do you see as my liabilities?" are both awesome questions. The answers direct us back to the soil of our own lives.

A mature Christianity is one that knows what is in the hearts of all people, but strange as it may seem, we are so made that we know the hearts of others only by looking into our own. When all is said and done, however, that is always an extraordinarily difficult work. We need all the help we can get. As Jeremiah pointed out, "The heart is more devious than any other thing, perverse too: who can pierce its secrets?" (Jer. 17:9 Jer.)

I would answer Jeremiah by saying that perhaps the heart's secrets can be pierced by the one who is willing to declare himself the patient, which usually takes more humility than most of us have, or more pain than most of us have allowed ourselves to acknowledge. Perhaps if we recognize this we can give ourselves to creating communities where wounded people are welcome and where all of us can find the courage to be about the hard work of knowing ourselves.

*Elizabeth*

P.S. This year I want to propose to our own small groups and other communities that they use New Year's Eve or New Year's Day as a time of reflection on the year gone and the year to come. We might give journal writing parties in our homes New Year's Eve and guide celebrants in a two-hour period of "journaling." The hour before the New Year could be used to share from our journals. A birthday or the anniversary of a relationship would also be occasions when individuals might want to work with this exercise. I would suggest the following questions for help in reflecting on the year:

How did the year begin? What were the events of winter? of spring? of summer? of fall?

What took place in your home relations? your work relations? your church relations? What events in the larger community of city, country and world most captured your attention?

Who were the significant people in your life? What books and art instructed your mind and heart?

Did you create anything this year? Did you make any new discoveries about yourself? How were you gift last year to a person, a community or an institution?

What was your greatest joy in this year gone? What was your greatest sorrow? What caused you the most disappointment? What caused you the most sadness?

In what areas of your life did you grow? Were these areas related to your joy or your pain?

What are your regrets? How would you do things differently, if you could live the year again? What did you learn?

Did you have a recurring dream? What theme or themes ran through your year?

Did you grow in your capacity to be a person in community—to bear your own burdens, to let others bear theirs? Did you have sufficient time apart with yourself?

Did you root your life more firmly in Scripture? Did you grow in your understanding of yourself? What was your most important insight? Did God seem near or far off?

What do you feel is the message of the year? What do you think and feel that God might be saying to you?

When Father Alfred Delp was in a Nazi prison awaiting the mock trial that announced his execution, he wrote in his journal: "...This year now ending leaves behind us a rich legacy of tasks, and we must seriously consider how to tackle them. Above all else, one thing is necessary—religious-minded people must become more devout; their dedication must be extended and intensified." What are the tasks that the old year leaves to you? How can you increase your devotion and dedication?

How do you want to create the new year? What kind of commitment do you want to make to yourself? Your community? To the oppressed people of the world? How do the questions about commitment make you feel? Angry? Challenged? Hopeful? What are your feelings?

Who are the people with whom you would like to deepen your relationships in the year to come? Do you have relationships that need to be healed? What can you do to heal your own heart? What can others do to assist in your healing? In Scripture it is written, "Ask and you shall receive." How can you ask God for what you need? How can you ask his people for what you need?

Is there a special piece of inward work that you would like to accomplish? Is there a special outward work? What are the goals that seem important to you? What are your hopes? What are your fears? What are the immediate first steps that you can take toward the goals that seem important to you?

After we have shared from our journals we might have a time of prayer in which to give thanks for all the events of the year gone, and to ask that the God through whose fingers they were filtered will continue to bless them to our use. They are now the bread of our life—part of all that we have to share with another when we share what is ours to give away. Our journal writing can help us to ring out the old year with our tears and gratitude, and to ring in the new year with praise and prayers of petition.

## NOTES

1. *Jung's Contribution to Our Time: The Collected Papers of Eleanor Bertine* (New York: G. P. Putnam's Sons for the C. G. Jung Foundation for Analytical Psychology, 1967), p. 122.
2. Martin Buber, *Ten Rungs: Hasidic Sayings* (New York: Schocken Books, 1947), p. 70.
3. Buber, *Ten Rungs: Hasidic Sayings* (New York: Schocken Books, 1947), p. 40.
4. W. H. Gardner, ed., *Gerald Manley Hopkins, Poems and Prose* (New York: Penguin Books, 1953). p. 141.
5. John D. Ingalls, *A Trainer's Guide to Andragogy* (City: U.S. Department of Health, Education, and Welfare, March, 1972), p. 172.

# 6

# ON OUR
# MULTIDIMENSIONAL
# NATURE

*Dear Sisters and Brothers:*

The over-arching theme of Paul's epistle to the Ephesians is the unity of the whole created order. We are knit and bonded to each other as our own bodies are knit and bonded together. I am not healthy if I have a sick leg or an ailing lung, and neither am I growing in love unless you are growing in love. I am not fully developing my gift unless you are exercising your gift. We are inextricably related to one another. My small group cannot fully do its work unless yours is doing its work. The hand needs the foot. The Seekers Church cannot fully build itself in love unless the Dayspring Church is fulfilling its given activity. The Church of the Saviour cannot accomplish its work unless The First Baptist Church and The Assembly of God Church are adding their strength. "The whole frame," says Ephesians, "grows through the due activity of each part. . ." (Eph. 4:16 NEB), and that includes the church in Johannesburg, Calcutta, and Mexico City, and on and on.

In Christ all the boundaries that separate me from you, one group from another group and one nation from another nation disappear. This is the mystery hidden in Christ that Paul with his spiritual genius perceived. The secret that he grasped was the wondrous secret of our unity. The people of God are those who are in on the secret, who inherit this vision of the unity, and who have, to use Paul's words, the privilege "of explaining how the mystery is to be dispensed." If we have truly grasped the secret with head and heart we are, ourselves, the "new creation" —the persons and groups between whom boundaries cease to exist.

A mature Christianity, then, is one in which an understanding of interrelatedness has come to full development. According to Ephesians the family is the prototype of the new society. Every husband is to love his wife as he loves himself, and every wife is to respect her husband. Parents are not to upset their children, and children are to honor their parents. The family is to illustrate how everyone in the church is to relate.

In the new society each member will count as each member of the family counts. Jesus asks, "Who is my mother? Who are my brothers?" And looking round at those who were sitting in the circle about him he said, "Here are my mother and my brothers. Whoever does the will  of God is my brother, my sister, my mother" (Mark 3:33–35 NEB). In the family-oriented Hebrew society that statement alone was a radical pronouncement of a new way of relating. The family models for the church, and the church for the world, the unity we have in Christ.

Do we see the whole of humanity being knit together into one seamless garment? Very rarely. There are few signs of a unifying work. This is why the heart of the world leapt up when Egyptian President Anwar Sadat went out from his country to meet with Prime Minister Menachem Begin, and the Israeli leader, completing the movement, went forward to greet him while his wildly excited people cheered and waved Egyptian flags. Even if all our hopes go down to defeat, for brief hours we overcame caution and wore our hearts upon our sleeves, shared common yearnings for peace, and witnessed upon one battlefield the embrace of enemies. We know better how we are to treat each other, especially the one we call enemy.

The world is dangerously schizophrenic. The divisions "out there" exist within our church communities and within ourselves. The family is breaking down under pressures too severe for it to handle. The society in which we live makes it difficult for parents to carry out their functions of parenting. The stability of the home is threatened by vocational insecurity, the threat of annihilation by nuclear warfare, a decline in morals, the breakdown of religions, crime in the streets, and the ever-present threat of cancer from the air we breathe, the food we eat, the clothes our children sleep in, the pills we take and the jobs we work at. The emphasis is not on love but on violence. Life does not flourish under these circumstances. Only when we feel cared for and safe does this happen, and then, and then only, does civilization flourish. Anxiety makes us all more self-centered and less aware of the neighbor.

Ours is not a time in which culture thrives. The world is flying apart. The churches cry peace where there is no peace. Small groups that have withdrawn from the organized church in an effort to be the church in the world and to live out the New Testament concept of koinonia—a shared life—find themselves exhausted by their efforts with not much "to show." The following letter which I quote in full bears witness to a dedication and sincerity of purpose that would be hard to match:

106 E. Wallace Ave.
New Castle, Pa. 16101
November 28, 1977

The Church of the Saviour
2025 Mass. Ave., NW
Washington, D.C., 20036

Dear Brothers and Sisters in Christ,

I am writing to inquire about the possibility of coming to live with your fellowship for a time. I am a partner with three other men in a Christian business. Over the past three years we have done painting, wallpapering, light carpentry, plumbing, cabinetry, remodeling, demolition, and salvage, etc. Our long-range goals include building housing for a developing Christian community. We have not made making a profit a primary goal of our business, rather we have sought to work with quality and integrity and to build skills in a semiprofessional way. Meanwhile we have just earned a living.

Our business family includes my wife and myself, our two children, two other married couples, one of whom has a child, and one single man. All of us are thirty and under.

The developing community we are a part of is centered in western Pennsylvania. Our fellowship has been very aware of the kind of church community and common life which you and your sister communities have been living in recent years. Many of us have been striving (sometimes in the flesh, I fear) to have that same unity in Christ. However, there are different ideas among us concerning what community is and how it is to be achieved. This has left us with many years of struggle, much psychic energy spent, and not much to show for it as far as some of us are concerned.

Some of us who feel that the fullness of koinonia and agape are not being realized in our fellowship feel that it may be wise to experience a fellowship like yours for a time and thereby possibly gain some wisdom, insight, and experience firsthand. We are not certain that the Lord will open doors in this direction but we wish to knock in hope.

In short, I am asking how your fellowship would feel about the possibility of receiving some or all of us to share and learn with you for approximately six months to a year in return for our labor in any building or renovations we may help you accomplish.

There are many factors, some of them difficult, which bear on our ability to come even if you might decide you would like to have us. Lord willing they can be worked out. We are sure you will want to know more about us before you can decide wisely. We will be prayerfully awaiting your preliminary response.

In Christ's love,
David Frengel

P.S. We have made this same inquiry to Reba Place in Chicago, Community of Celebration in Colorado, and Grace and Peace in St. Louis, who along with your fellowship seem to us to offer real hope for growth in service to Christ. If there are others which you feel may offer some possibility, please feel free to pass this letter on. Thank you.

One would like to answer such a letter by writing, "Yes, come and be with us. We offer ourselves as mature guides in the building of koinonia. If you touch the community here, you will see how we love one another." But alas, our own community is riddled with complaints, conflict, competition, anger, jealousy and infidelity. We have people who want to belong and feel left out, others who hate their jobs and find their lives meaningless, or who lack confidence in themselves and do not know what they are to do in life. At the other end of the pole are those who are very certain of the way to go, and want their own way in everything.

A minister recently said to me, "Your books seem heavy, and full of pain." And I replied, "You read well." Jean Vanier began a lecture at Georgetown University with the words, "It is a terrible, terrible, terrible world out there." Two rows behind me listening to those words was Rose Kennedy, mother of a retarded daughter, of another daughter killed in a plane crash, of a son killed in war, of two murdered sons and of a grandchild maimed by cancer—and these were only a few public facts. But I had more than Rose Kennedy's life to reflect on. I had my own, and those of my friends.

Despite the fact that we are visited by disease and attacked by nature, most of our suffering comes from our not knowing how to relate to each other, how to stand on our own feet or how to help others bear their burdens. We think that community can be built in a few years, if not a few nights, and wonder "what is wrong with us" or "with them" when the community that we are given to nurture and sustain does not live up to our expectations. We never question that those expectations might be unreal and stand in the way of community.

If the sublime words of Ephesians are true, and everyone on the earth is of one family with one Mother and one Father—if we are indeed joint heirs—then the task of a mature Christianity is to deal with the blocks that prevent our communion and our sharing. Recently when Gordon Cosby was talking about the split between what the churches proclaim from their pulpits and what they live out in their structures, he touched on two of the blocks that prevent our participating in the unifying work of Christ: One is our not really knowing in any fundamental way that we belong to the totality of Christ's body, which in turn is related to the whole human family.

We have not grasped in any deep measure the message of the Gospels. We view ourselves in an individualistic way rather than perceiving that our destiny is bound up with the destiny of each of the sister communities. If one is having trouble, we all are in trouble. Just as one unfulfilled, frustrated child can wreak havoc in a family, so one segment that lacks identity and does not know its servant path can fragment an institution. If one part is doing well, its health strengthens us all. We belong to each other, and we belong to the Church—to St. James' Catholic Church and The First Church of the Nazarene, to the church in South Africa, in Brazil, in India, in Australia—wherever it is. We also belong to the people of General Motors, of San Quentin prison, the Pentagon and Public School 81. This belonging is harder to understand. Nevertheless, the word is that "There is only Christ: he is everywhere and he is in everything" (Col. 3:11 Jer.).

A second point that Gordon made was that it is essential that the body constantly move out to create a unity. This was the commission of Jesus, "Go forth therefore and make all nations my disciples. . ." (Matt. 28:19 NEB). Introduce them into the mystery that you see in me. This is the very point that Paul was making in Ephesians.

But how do we get across to our neighbors the unity that permeates the whole created order? This is everyone's assignment—the deepening of our relationship with God and the deepening of our relationship with each other. We are to create new possibilities for the sharing of ourselves. The leader is out there doing that. He is the one, she is the one, who is trying to reconcile the differences as Christ reconciled the differences in himself. The work of the leader is the healing of the divisions. "What blocks the leader," Gordon said, "is that when he emerges we take shots at him. We wound him, we make it difficult for him to do his work."

He was quoting from a much longer statement by Jean Vanier:

> Many people coming to community begin projecting onto the leader or leaders some of their own difficulties with their parents. Then they go into dichotomy of aggressiveness-servility. That's to say, they can become alternately very aggressive toward the leader and then terribly servile. They obey, and then—boom. They don't meet the leader as a person, which may be partly the fault of the leader, not meeting the other as a person.
>
> Leaders make good targets for people's aggressions. What hap-

pens sometimes is that people push the leader higher up on the pedestal, because then there's a better target. They never quite knock you down though. That's dangerous. They know that somebody else will have to go up there—and they don't want to take the job. So they wound you in the leg, not in the heart.

My guess is that both Gordon Cosby and Jean Vanier were speaking out of their own experience. Of course, the same treatment will be the lot of any one of us who is acknowledged as a leader, unless the members of our communities are earnestly about the work of trying to discern their projections. Until we become more conscious, which is what spiritual growth is about, we will make it difficult for our leaders to lead. This consciousness is primarily a matter of each person's knowing what her gift is and exercising it for the building of the whole. People do not know, or forget to mention, that this is one of the basic conditions for any sense of unity or communion between persons. If they were aware of this one condition of community they would talk about community in a different way. Actually, community exists to the extent that each person is free to be himself and to grow toward his full potential. This implies a condition of acceptance which is extraordinarily difficult to give and to receive.

Another important block to our understanding each other and sensing the unity of the world is our failure to develop a unity within ourselves—an inner integrity that ministers to our total being. The great spiritual director, Baron Friedrich von Hügel, said that a full and mature religion contains a creative tension between the mystical or emotional element, the historical or institutional element, and the intellectual or scientific element. Douglas V. Steere, the Quaker leader, commented, "The spiritual guide who will speak to the soul's real need must teach it the place of each of these elements in a full religious diet or ration. . . . "[1]

Actually the need for humans to care for and nourish their multidimensional nature has been recognized by spiritual leaders from many different religious traditions. Despite this, neither spiritual directors nor educators give very much attention to our varied nature, which may account in large part for the reason that there is so little peace in the world. We have all grown up a bit lopsided. More than any other reason this might account for the difficulty we have in communicating with each other, and in understanding viewpoints different from our own. It makes for conflict within us and between us.

The person whose intellectual center is well developed looks at the world through a different window than the one who is looking at the world through a more highly developed emotional center. It is the same world, but each sees different aspects. This failure to achieve anything approximating equal development of all the centers accounts for much of the discontent in small group life.

A person developed in his or her intellectual center will complain in this manner, "The trouble with this group is that it has no stimulating study. We need to cut our teeth on theology, study the theologians and know what the different schools of thought are." The person weighted on the side of the historical might reply, "No, the difficulty with this group is that it is not grounded in tradition. We need to steep ourselves in the Scriptures and celebrate the Eucharist when we meet." The emotionally oriented person will interject, "The trouble with us is that we do not give opportunity for clapping hands, for wailing and tears, for praising the Lord with dance and timbrel."

Listening in on these discussions I have sometimes been reminded of the charge that Gordon Cosby gives to the couples he marries: "I charge each of you to grow to that place where each derives major satisfaction from giving satisfaction to the other." It is a fit charge to give the members of any community.

We must sacrifice for each other our illusions—in this case the illusion that our view of a given situation is necessarily the correct one. For any of us such a sacrifice is really a remarkable accomplishment, so immersed are we in our own view of things. If we were to train ourselves—and it does require training—to be open to what another has to say, perhaps the bones of sleeping selves would be stirred. Those undeveloped countries within would tap in on their resources. In mystical literature we might enter upon the fourth way. Instead of looking through one pane, one comes out from behind his window and views the whole scene, looking with the whole of himself. In Christian terms this is growing up into the full stature of Christ.

When we began to worship together as The Eighth Day

Church, we agreed to take turns preaching. We very quickly discovered that our reactions to any given person may differ widely. One will say, "So-and-so is preaching today. I must let this person and that person know." Another responds with, "How I wish I could stay home." I have been accused of being too heavily weighted on the side of the emotional. "Psychological" is another description for those with my emphasis. I have pondered this in myself. I think that it is undoubtedly true. But could it be that I am forced into my role in order to right the balance in our corporate life? If others took the task of addressing this dimension of our being, would I be more free to choose another emphasis?

In one of his books Carl Jung talks about a man who was known as a saint. Jung said that he found it hard to believe until he met the man's wife. She was irritable and ugly and very obviously living out her husband's shadow. I have seen this in cases where the husband will be very down to earth, and the wife completely unconcerned about the practical details of life. Obviously as long as she fails to deal with the concrete, he has to make up for it, or their household does not survive.

I once belonged to a group comprised of seven members, all of whom except one were very open and supportive of everything that I said. That one continually questioned and fought every creative adventure and innovative approach I proposed. He called himself a liberal and I called him a conservative. I looked forward to his leaving the group but, to my amazement, when he did, I felt myself no longer free to soar. I began putting a check on my spontaneous enthusiasm. I became my own critic. I had to, or run the risk of directing our energies down a course that was unexamined and untested by the conflict of minds. I missed my enemy, now grown so dear, who had done this work for me.

Our beings cry out for balance, and when we do not achieve it within ourselves, we manipulate others into achieving it for us, and usually end up disliking in them this projected dimension of ourselves. Part of us knows that we have given away what belongs to us. The recipients are not happy either. They are carrying responsibilities not rightfully theirs.

One of the first people to speak at our Potter's House was a

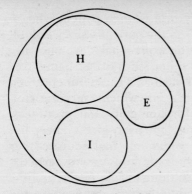

An Historically Developed Person

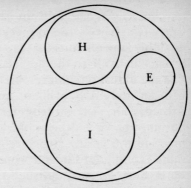

An Intellectually Developed Person

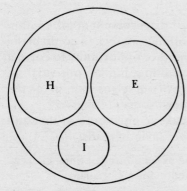

An Emotionally Developed Person

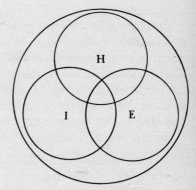

A Kingdom Person

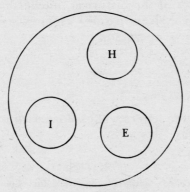

A Pigmy Person

psychoanalyst. She told the story of a woman patient who, at thirty-two, had "gone to pieces." As the patient's story unfolded, it became obvious that the young woman had developed her intellectual side to the neglect of other sides of her being. She was the oldest daughter, a bit awkward as a child, but endowed with an extremely brilliant mind, a gift which everyone confirmed. Her sister, recognized for her gaity and prettiness, became known as "the popular one," the party girl. To keep her place in the family structure the older one had educated her mind, competed for and won scholastic honors and earned a Ph.D. She had accomplished these things while neglecting the development of the gifts of her feminine self—tenderness and caring. The imbalance so weakened her whole world that it collapsed.

This might be a lesson to us in the discernment of gifts within our small mission groups. We so often are quick to confirm the obvious, rather than giving to each other opportunity to correct the imbalance in ourselves by developing hidden potential. In the neglected or inferior dimension of ourselves is often hid the seed of the new person and the new future.

A line in the commitment we make as members of the faith communities of The Church of the Saviour reads:

> I commit myself, regardless of the expenditures of time, energy and money to becoming an informed mature Christian.

Surely that commitment includes our growing in recognition and appreciation of the historical, intellectual and emotional dimensions of ourselves. In time we may even come to know out of which center we speak and listen.

*Elizabeth*

P.S. My next three letters will explore each of these three aspects of our lives.

### NOTES

1. Douglas V. Steere, ed., *Spiritual Counsel and Letters of Baron Friedrich von Hügel* (New York: Harper and Row, Publishers, Inc., 1964), p. 8.

# 7

# *ON* OUR
# HISTORICAL
# CENTER

*Dear Brothers and Sisters:*

In my last letter I wrote that the nurture of our multidimentional being is essential if we are to know an inner unity that will nurture unity in the world. This letter singles out the historical center, which is often more neglected than either the emotional or intellectual center.

For all of us the historical has three major aspects: our individual history, our history as the people of God and our history as a member of the human race. Perhaps the best way to educate the historical element in ourselves is to draw close to our own individual history. As was indicated in an earlier letter, the journal is a most useful tool for doing this. Therapeutic programs are another. In actuality they offer a time specifically structured for reflection on one's past. The most intense of such reflections occurs during psychoanalysis which attempts to integrate not only the remembered past, but the forgotten past. One psychoanalyst put it this way, "To those who cannot look ahead, I must ask that they look back."

The strange thing is that the person who is not acquainted with her past has little sense of the future, and is therefore unable to live fully in the present. This may explain the quest of adopted children for lost parents. They do not need those parents to be spiritual and psychological mothers and fathers. They usually have these. They want to look into the faces of their biological parents because they need to know their history.

If we are to have relationships with friends that are high and deep and broad and long, we will have to become better acquainted with their stories as well as our own. I was made aware of this again last week when in a class in Christian Growth members shared their responses to the question, "What was it like to grow up in your parents' house?" We grew close not only to the past but to each other. I was reminded of a therapist who, in telling his own story as a healer, was quoted as saying, "I am convinced that I will love anyone I come to know."

Another way of stating this is to say that if we do not love the members of our faith communities the reason may be that we have not heard their stories. We usually do not ask each other that most historical of all questions, "What was it like when you were small?" All their lives, children need to be encouraged to ask that question of their parents, and parents need to be encouraged to tell their stories to their children.

By asking persons in our communities to write their spiritual autobiographies and to read them for the members of their small groups, we help them to identify God's mighty works in their individual histories. In the past ten years no one has come into the membership of The Church of the Saviour without reading his story for the council, which is now made up of two members from each of our six communities. We will do well to continue this tradition, and to be alert for other appropriate story-telling hours. In my community we recently celebrated the thirteenth birthday of Brett Holt and took the occasion to give each member an opportunity to say what was the most important memory of his or her own thirteenth year.

The need to tell our stories is often strong upon us during transition periods. These are the times when one is being prepared for a new thrust into the future. That thrust cannot be made with power unless it is fully integrated with the past.

The aged, whose futures are wrapped in the most awesome mystery, are in the most demanding of all transition stages. They need good listeners, who can help them go back over the years, review old accounts and take care of unfinished business. If we can be those listeners, we will gain a heart of wisdom. Simone de Beauvoir gives us this same message in her book, *The Coming of Age,* when she recounts a legend of the people of an Indonesian island:

> In Bali it is said that once upon a time the people of a remote mountain village used to sacrifice and eat their old men. A day came when there was not a single old man left, and the traditions were lost. They wanted to build a great house for the meetings of the assembly, but when they came to look at the tree trunks that had been cut for that purpose no one could tell the top from the bottom: If the timber were placed the wrong way up, it would set off a series of disasters. A young man said that if they promised never to eat the old men anymore, he would be able to find a solution. They promised. He brought his grandfather, whom he had hidden; and the old man taught the community to tell top from bottom.[1]

Our culture is still about the business of eating the old. Though we do it in less direct ways, our ways are neither more civilized nor less cruel. Only the wealthy, and very few of them, escape the severe deprivations that are the lot of the aged in America and many of the advanced countries. When we turn from the needs of the old, we estrange ourselves from our own future. Our concern with the past will then become a sign of regression, rather than an act of reflection.

The second aspect of the historical is our story as the people of God. Sarah suckled me. My father? He was a "wandering Aramaean." When Matthew gives the genealogy of Christ, and he takes pains to do so, he begins with Abraham. Luke is more universal in scope and takes us back to Adam, the head of the human race. Saint Paul is forever reminding the early Christian communities that their story begins in the land of the Pharoahs. Nor is Paul hesitant to tell the young churches his own story.

In joining the Christian Church we make commitment not only to one another, but to Abraham and Sarah, to Moses, Isaiah, Paul, Joan of Arc, Brother Lawrence, Dietrich Bonhoeffer, Martin Luther King, Thomas Merton—the church triumphant, and to the long line that will come after us—the church militant. We are, as Ephesians states, "part of a building that has the apostles and prophets for its foundations, and Christ Jesus himself for its main cornerstone" (Eph. 2:20 Jer.).

In our consideration of the historical let us not forget that the institutional counterpart of the people of God is the church. If teachings, concepts, experience and discoveries are to endure, be built upon and passed on, they must be protected. This the institution does for us. The founders (Mary and Gordon Cosby) of our own church community were free to begin The Church of the Saviour outside the denominational framework and to experiment with new servant structures, because if they failed in their quest, the institutional church was there to conceive new efforts, as well as to oppose them.

Baron von Hügel wrote:

> Never has religion been purely and entirely individual; always has it been, as truly and necessarily, social and institutional, traditional and historical. And this traditional element, not all the religious genius in the world can ever escape or replace: It was there, surrounding and moulding the very prenatal existence of each one of us; it will be there, long after we have left the scene. We live and die its wise servants and stewards, or its blind slaves, or in futile, impoverishing revolt against it: We never, for good or for evil, really get beyond its reach.[2]

Commenting on the place that von Hügel gave to the "hair shirt of some form of institutional religion," Douglas V. Steere wrote:

> Deep as is his respect for the spiritual and social witness of the Quakers, von Hügel is never tired of reminding them that they lack a deep enough sense of gratitude for the Bible, for the saints, and for the preservation of the active and regular confrontation by the historical Christ which has come down through history in the Church. For him, this regular confrontation of the worshiper by the historic Christ is an essential, and the Church is the tarnished mounting in which the jewel of Christ is set.
>
> His own view of the Church was naturally closely bound up with sacramental practice. There is something moving in the reports of scholarly companions who occasionally accompanied him on his daily walk on Hampstead Heath. One has spoken of how they were passing the little Catholic chapel on the Heath just as he was making some devastatingly critical remarks on a New Testament text, and

how he hastily excused himself, entered the chapel, sank down on his knees before the sacrament on the altar, and lost himself in prayer. For him there was apparently no incongruity between the free mind and scrupulous adherence to devotional practice. One of his happiest remarks referred to those who were very firm at the center, being able to be quite free at the periphery.[3]

In our six new church communities we discuss from time to time the structures that have evolved out of our life these past thirty years, and indicate that it might be well to replace them with new ones. Now and then those that we suggest putting in their place are the ones that, when we started our journey together, we put aside saying that they blocked our living out the message we were proclaiming. We would do well to heed George Santayana's warning, "He who does not know history is fated to repeat it."

If we can begin to nurture the historical dimension in ourselves we will be better able to grasp humankind's several-million-year history. Christianity is just 2,000 years old. Science is only a few hundred years old. Psychoanalysis is 100 years old. Our Church of the Saviour structures are thirty years old, and our new communities are three years old.

To the impatient ones of his day who were complaining that things have not changed and that everything is going on in the same old way despite the promise, Peter says, "But there is one thing, my friends, that you must never forget: that with the Lord 'a day' can mean a thousand years, and *a thousand years is like a day*. The Lord is not being slow to carry out his promises, as anybody else might be called slow; but he is patient with you all, wanting nobody to be lost and everybody to be brought to change his ways" (2 Pet. 3:8–10 Jer.). Within one sentence Peter illustrates the law of the opposites. We have all the time we need—"a thousand years is like a day." On the other hand, one day is as a thousand years.

Without an historical view we will despair of transformation. Change appears slow in us all and slower still in institutions, a condition that we all rage against from time to time, but one which we might find hard-pressed to improve upon. In this, as in other parts of the human design, one catches a glimpse of the mind of God at work. Consider, if you will, what it would be like, if we could easily change ourselves and our institutions. Without obstacles to overcome, would we feel our strength and aliveness, or an internal imperative to give our lives any painstaking care? In a situation where everything was subject to fast change, we could quickly pull out a disagreeable habit and insert some envied virtue. Of course, less worthy objectives could be as easily achieved. Furthermore, being creatures of impulse and irrationalities, as well as lovers of variety, we would surely find ourselves doing over our lives and institutions as readily as we now rearrange the furniture of a room.

More than this, with fast change available to us, we would end up with no intricately wrought internal structure. We would all be in danger of coming "unglued." Mentors and society would have influenced countless changes in each of us, if not imposed them, and we, ourselves, would have obeyed so many of our own good and ignoble impulses that it would be impossible to trace our roots, find out what made us what we are, or even know who we are or where we are going. Any integrative work would be foolish to attempt. Our institutions, always in the throes of change, would be undependable and unpredictable. More horrifying, friends who stayed apart too long would not find anything "in common" when they met, if indeed they recognized one another. We would all become mad persons crying down the streets of the world for help.

To be sure, we and our institutions are slow to change (which is hard to bear when feelings hurt and institutions are oppressive, and we need to change and be changed) but, when we reflect upon it, would we want fast change in ourselves or others? In any case, we have no choice but to struggle for change, remembering that with God a thousand years is as a day—remembering also that there is a terrible urgency. He who is our God, will come swiftly. All that is not holy will disintegrate in flames. Jesus is the ice, and he is the fire.

The third aspect of the historical is our pilgrimage as members of the human race. My own appreciation of that dimension was deepened by the story that a retreat leader told of a small fish which was washed up on a shore, and whose plight gave him three choices. One, he could just give up and die, two, he could try to make it back to the sea, and three, he could try to breathe. He chose to breathe and became the first lung fish. That lung fish gives me an emotional link with my origin. Loren Eiseley wrote: "The salt of those ancient seas is in our blood. Its lime is in our bones. Every time we walk along a beach some ancient urge disturbs us so that we find ourselves shedding shoes and garments, or scavenging among seaweed and whitened timbers like the homesick refugees of a long war."[4]

My consideration of the little lung fish does more than deepen my connection with the ancient seas that tossed me up. It puts me in touch with the evolutionary vocation that each of us has, as well as the realization that we have no assurance that humankind is necessarily here forever. Our species is threatened by our failure to develop our reflective powers. A recent issue of *Time Magazine* carried a seven-page story of man's ascent, citing the work of Richard Leakey, the anthropologist. Like his famous father, Leakey is spending his life in search of man's origins which, in turn, have directed his attention to the present and the future. The article ends with these arresting paragraphs, which oddly enough are a pure expression of Christianity:

Richard Leakey's life work, in fact, has made him impatient with those of narrow ethnic and national perspectives. He makes it clear to all that he is a Kenyan and proud to be a citizen of that African nation. Furthermore, he notes that racial differences, as they are commonly perceived, are a superficial and recent development, having arisen only about 15,000 years ago. Says Leakey: "I am aghast that people think they are different from each other. We all share a tremendous heritage, an exciting bond. We are all the same."

Leakey has learned another object lesson from his probes into the past. Increasingly concerned about overpopulation, environmental abuses and the depletion of natural resources, he fears that man may not be able to cope biologically, that he cannot genetically change fast enough to survive the ever-more-hostile environment he is creating. Says he: "People feel that we are here by predestination and that because we are humans we will be able to survive even if we make mistakes." But, cautions Leakey, these people have no perspective on the fact that humans are living organisms. "There have been thousands of living organisms," he says, "of which a very high percentage has become extinct. There is nothing, at the moment, to suggest that we are not part of the same pattern." He notes that there is one point of difference: man is the only organism with power to reflect on its past and upon its future. That power to reflect, he says, "is what makes us able to plan our future in such a way as to avoid what seems inevitable."[5]

In my own reflection I like to consider all the millions of fish tossed up on primordial shores who died making an effort to breathe, and became the vanguard of the small lung fish. It gives perspective to our own small efforts which so often seem to count for nothing when in actuality no expression of goodness, no gentle glance or breathed prayer is ever wasted. Peter's words make more sense than we seem to know:

> Look eagerly for the coming of the Day of God and work to hasten it on; that day will set the heavens ablaze until they fall apart, and will melt the elements in flames. But we have his promise, and look forward to new heavens and a new earth, the home of justice.
>
> (2 Pet. 3:12–13 NEB)

In his letter the Apostle Peter divides history into three sections or worlds: the world that has been covered by the Flood, the tragic world in which we presently exist and the world with its new heavens and new earth which is to come. In Peter we see a man whose experience and sense of the past was linked to his anticipation of the future. The backward glance combined with the forward look enabled him to live as a man of hope in his own tragic time. So it was with Teilhard de Chardin, the Jesuit priest and anthropologist, who believed that any goodness hastened the coming of the New Age. And so with us, the nurturing of the historical center will give urgency to our own acts of goodness which will be caught up by God and used in the "universal restoration."

## NOTES

1. (New York: G. P. Putnam's Sons, 1972), p. 77.
2. *Spiritual Counsel and Letters of Baron Friedrich von Hügel*, p. 133.
3. *Spiritual Counsel*, p. 27.
4. *The Unexpected Universe* (New York: Harcourt, Brace & World Inc., 1963), p. 51.
5. "Puzzling Out Man's Ascent," *Time Magazine* (November 7, 1977), p. 78.

# 8

# ON OUR
# INTELLECTUAL
# CENTER

*Dear Sisters and Brothers:*

To commit one's self to becoming an informed, mature Christian means more than an historical awareness of God's acting in the long cycles of history and our own history. The historical dimension by itself is not capable of nurturing our thrust into the future. With too heavy an emphasis on the historical our religion would be full of cobwebs, musty and yellowed with no fresh breezes stirring. We all know institutions and persons like that. All their windows nailed shut, and everywhere the feel of death.

Becoming a mature Christian also means to be intellectually alive, open to new thought and in pursuit of truth. Charles Darwin's story has a large claim on me for the instruction it gives in living; perhaps, also, because he knew a harsh rejection. In his narrative so safely removed from us, we see how unsettling thought is. Also, the young Darwin, who was to become so single-minded, had trouble finding out what he was to do in life, and that makes some of us with the same trouble feel more acceptable. As a boy he had a passion for gardening, animals, beaches, flying birds, and for collecting rocks, flowers and crawling things. A patron of gifts would have noted and nurtured these loves in the youth, but his father who was a successful doctor wanted his son "to follow in his footsteps," an error not uncommon among fathers and mentors, but one which, nonetheless, makes it extraordinarily difficult for the young to hear the Voice that transcends human voices. Darwin, who was so eager to please, though fated not to please, went dutifully to Edinburgh to study medicine. His biographer, Alan Moorehead,[1] upon whom I rely heavily in relating Darwin's story, reports that the sight of blood made him ill, and that he was allowed to abandon medicine and go to Cambridge to prepare for the ministry, a vocation that had no strong attraction, but one which his father felt to be respectable, and one which the young Charles could comtemplate with some ease. As a minister in a country parish he would have time to pursue his collecting hobby. It did not occur to him that what he loved doing was what he *"ought"* to do.

At Cambridge he succeeded no better than at Edinburgh— but he made friends with Professor Henslow who taught botany. Henslow is an example of Erik Erikson's "generative" man— the one who cares about the young and the kind of future they will have. He saw in Darwin a gifted naturalist and became an evoker and encourager of his gifts. He took him as companion on nature walks and boat rides, and invited him to lectures and discussion groups that further stimulated his interest in the natural world and put him in the company of men of science. All the while Darwin earned a proper degree, though it is very unlikely that he would have measured up to the standards of today's universities.

When Henslow was not able to accept an invitation to the post of unpaid naturalist aboard Her Majesty's Ship, The Beagle, he recommended to the young Captain Robert FitzRoy that he invite Darwin, which he did. Though he had never considered himself a naturalist, Darwin was thrilled with the invitation. Not so his father. Moorehead writes of the father's response,

> Dr. Darwin had other views. He thought it was a wild scheme; Charles had already switched from medicine and now he was running away from the Church; he was not used to the sea and would be away for two years or more; he would be uncomfortable; he would never settle down after he got back; he would harm his repu-

tation as a serious clergyman; others must have been offered the post before him, and since they had refused there must be something fishy about it; in short, a useless undertaking.[2]

The authoritative father, who also held the purse strings, did say, however, "If you can find any man of common sense who advises you to go I will give my consent."[3] Once again Darwin, standing in need of an advocate, found one in an uncle, who was able to forcefully state that it was too good an opportunity to miss. The captain of the good ship The Beagle had more than routine scientific inquiries in mind. He was a missionary captain in search of competent evidence that would establish by proof the biblical account of the early beginning of man and of the Flood. In many ways Darwin appeared an ideal recruit for such a mission. He was an acute observer of natural history and a clergyman-to-be who shared FitzRoy's belief in a literal interpretation of Scripture. Darwin reveled in the world, had little desire to change it, wanted to see more of it, and as always was eager to please.

Stage by stage, The Beagle made its voyage, and stage by stage an untold world unfolded before Darwin's eyes. Whenever the boat anchored he would be off on a new exploration—observing, taking notes, collecting. In between moorings, he laid his new collections out on the deck and did the work of "dissecting, classifying and making notes." Other specimens that began to include teeth, bones and skeletons he packed up and sent back home to Professor Henslow. For a long time he clung to the hope of making the discoveries that would satisfy his captain, but something was interfering. As one biographer wrote, Darwin was looking at what every man before him had looked at, and thinking thoughts no one had ever thought before.

As he became more open and questioning, Captain Robert FitzRoy became more closed and hardened. He told Darwin that there were things we were not meant to understand. It was too late for Darwin to hear the fearful and cautionary words. He had eaten of forbidden fruit. He could not turn back. The paradise of his own innocence was forever lost. Behind him was a gate and over it a cherubim and flashing swords. He had begun to explore the ideas of evolution that would eventually lead him to the conclusion that the story of Adam and Eve was a myth.

His thoughts were all the more disturbing because there was no representative of the church on hand to let him know that myths hold the deepest truths of humankind. Surely a terrible war went on in him before the story of the origins of man that family and church had handed down were abandoned for the never-before-told saga that was unfolding on the decks of The Beagle. In his own biography he wrote, "disbelief crept over me at a very slow rate but was at last complete." The warm, considerate and gentle Darwin was in possession of findings that in Victorian England would make him a social outcast.

There is no more fearful thing in all the world than to hold convictions different from those of one's community, so quick are we to make "outsiders" of anyone who does not see things the way we see them. Darwin left The Beagle, and kept his silence for twenty years, during which time he suffered ill health. Through all those silent and turbulent years Henslow remained his friend and enthusiastic supporter, securing a grant toward the writing of a five-volume work on the zoology of The Beagle.

Finally in 1859 Darwin published his book entitled, *On the Origin of Species by Means of Natural Selection, or the Preservation of Favoured Races in the Struggle of Life.* A threatened and outraged clergy raised their voices in protest. In the words of an archbishop they were out to "smash Darwin."

Educators were no less bitter. In his book *Darwin's Century,* Loren Eiseley quotes President Barnard of Columbia University as saying:

> If the final outcome of all the boasted discoveries of modern science is to disclose to men that they are more evanescent than the shadow of the swallow's wing upon the lake. . .give me then, I pray, no more science. I will live on in my simple ignorance, as my fathers did before me. . . .[4]

We all say that the truth will set us free, but when the view of life that has given us meaning appears in jeopardy, few of us find the faith to affirm that a more life-enhancing view will be given in its place. Eiseley writes:

...The evolutionists discovered that nature "makes things make themselves" and thus succeeded in apparently removing the need for a Master Craftsman. The resulting excitement was so great that it was only later that the question began to be asked: Why *does* nature let things make themselves? Obviously this is a question science can only philosophize about but cannot answer. It can trace the organism down to the final cell; it may even be able someday, in its knowledge of biophysics and chemistry, to create simple life, but it will still not be able to answer the final why. For at that point science will have left the field of secondary causes in which it operates so successfully and, instead, will be asking the primary and unanswerable questions.[5]

No one states more eloquently than Loren Eiseley the message of unity that Charles Darwin bequeathed to us. These are the last paragraphs of his book:

...As a young man somewhere in the high starred Andean night, or perhaps drinking alone at an island spring where wild birds who had never learned to fear man came down upon his shoulder, Charles Darwin saw a vision. It was one of the most tremendous insights a living being ever had. It combined the awful roar of Hutton's Scottish brook with a glimpse of Smith's frail ladder dangling into the abyss of vanished eras. None of his forerunners has left us such a message; none saw, in a similar manner, the whole vista of life with quite such sweeping vision. None, it may be added, spoke with the pity which infuses these lines: *If we choose to let conjecture run wild, then animals, our fellow brethren in pain, disease, suffering and famine—our slaves in the most laborious works, our companions in our amusements—they may partake of our origin in one common ancestor—we may be all melted together.*"[6]
Darwin was twenty-eight when he jotted down this paragraph in his notebook. If he had never conceived of natural selection, if he had never written the *Origin,* it would still stand as a statement of almost clairvoyant perception. There are very few youths today who will pause, coming from a biology class, to finger a yellow flower or poke in friendly fashion at a sunning turtle on the edge of the campus pond, and who are capable of saying to themselves, "We are all one—all melted together." It is for this, as much as for the difficult, concise reasoning of the *Origin,* that Darwin's shadow will run a long way forward into the future.

In the end, when all the facts are in, Darwin's message turns out to be the message hidden in Christ—the message of the unity of the whole created order.

If to some Darwin seemed to be introducing material that discredited traditional ways of relating to biblical truths, for others a fresh wind was blowing. These folk had probably long been plagued by their own disturbing thoughts. Unfortunately in the years to come many of them would exit from the church leaving organized religion to its emotions and a boneyard history.

In those years not so very long ago began the split between science and religion. You will note that the scientific is the counterpart of the intellectual element of religion, as the institutional is the counterpart of the historical. If our faith were not so small, we would not have to silence a Darwin, or send a Teilhard de Chardin into exile. Science could be put under the feet of Christ where all things belong.

Another revolutionary thinker that the church still treats as an outcast is Sigmund Freud. His unpopularity among believers is due in large part to his views on religion. Despite our doctrine of forgiveness we have not been able to forgive him for not saying nicer things about us.

Freud clearly illustrates that when we disagree with a portion of a man's thinking we are inclined to reject the whole body of his work, and sometimes even the man himself. The revolutionary doctor gave his life to discovering and lifting up to the light disguised and hidden forces that are at work in us all. He gave us his research and findings as free gift, but we failed to interpret them theologically either for him, a son of God, or for the body of believers, although this was the job of the church. We claimed to be healers, but he did not see us engaged in the work of healing. Never has anyone been more committed to the doctrine of original sin than Sigmund Freud. In fact, he was so immersed in that concept that it may have eclipsed for him the doctrine of man made in God's image. This is not to say that Sigmund Freud was without a pastor/prophet relationship. In October of 1918 his friend, the Reverend Oskar Pfister, wrote to him:

...Finally you ask why psychoanalysis was not discovered by any of the pious, but by an atheist Jew. The answer obviously is that piety is not the same as genius for discovery and that most of the pious did not have it in them to make such discoveries. Moreover, in the first place you are no Jew, which to me, in view of my unbounded admiration for Amos, Isaiah, Jeremiah, and the author of Job and Ecclesiastes, is a matter of profound regret, and in the second place you are not godless, for he who lives the truth lives in God, and he who strives for the freeing of love "dwelleth in God" (First Epistle of John, iv, 16). If you raised to your consciousness and fully felt your place in the great design, which to me is as necessary as the synthesis of the notes is to a Beethoven symphony, I should say to you: A better Christian there never was. . . .[7]

The published letters of Pfister and Freud confirm the caring relationship between the man of cloth and the man of the new healing art.

Freud, however, did more than misunderstand the nature of the church. He wrote to Fliess, a companion in discovery, "We are terribly ahead of our time." His fear was not ungrounded. He tried to teach us things we did not want to learn and caused himself as well as his contemporaries no small amount of anxiety. Esther Dorsey told me of listening in on the conversation of two small nieces playing school with a friend. Lisa, the oldest, was in the role of teacher and stood before the smaller ones saying, "Now children, I want you to know that there is no Easter bunny. Do you understand? There is no Easter bunny." The information was too much for her sister who stamped her feet angrily on the floor, and cried out in her dismay, "Lisa, you are teaching us things we do not want to learn."

We all vaguely sense that we have cherished illusions about ourselves and about the world that we might have to give up if we learn too much. We do not usually stamp our feet and shake our fists, but quite often we fall into a common state of being asleep in life.

Robert Coles, the writer and psychoanalyst, tells a lovely story of Erik Erikson's encounter with President Heuss of the East German Republic.[8] The occasion was the 100th anniversary of Sigmund Freud's birth. Erikson was to deliver the principal address at a celebration given jointly by the universities of Heidelberg and Frankfort. Before the address the very old Heuss confided to Erikson that he felt strange introducing him since he had some reservations about Freud's ideas. "Frankly," he told Erikson, "if I look into myself I can notice absolutely nothing demonic. And you know, I don't think I ever had any infantile sexuality." Coles reports that Erikson replied, "Presidents don't need that kind of thing." President Heuss said gratefully, "Thank you, thank you," and together they walked toward the academic procession. A little while later President Heuss introduced Erikson and then promptly fell asleep.

I like that story, not only because it illustrates how we protect ourselves, ask for comfort and receive it, but because when I am tempted to "set straight" people with opposing viewpoints, Erikson comes to mind as a gentle, more humble and accepting way to be in the world. I long for myself that generosity of spirit, and have come to feel that we lack it most when we are repressing or rejecting elements in ourselves that we are afraid to recognize. When I feel superior, or sound condemning or moralistic, I have reason to wonder what parts of myself are not being authentically experienced. What idealized image of myself am I clinging to? What are the more genuine feelings that I am afraid to express? What are the thoughts that I fear to claim as my own?

My mind wanders along these paths because I continue to find my spirit and mind fed and enlarged by the writings of men and women who have no relationship with the church and for whom it does not exist in any important way. Most of the giants in the field of depth psychology are not Christians or, if they are, they do not feel good about mentioning it. I want my friends to read them because I feel that they can help us to be persons in community, confirm gifts and be healers. The fact that the authors have another lifestyle and contradict some of our important values is not sufficient reason for cutting off a dialogue, or for failing to sit at the feet of those who have things to teach us. The contemplative can best be described as the one who has been enough in the silence to be aware of his own poverty and lack of answers. One of our communities calls itself The Seekers. That seems so good, for it defines the church not as the people with the answers—the ones who will tell you what to think and what to do—but as the people who will be our companions on a search.

The Eighth Day Church was sometimes asked why the foreign students in the polycultural education program it sponsored were not required to be Christian. I do not know what was behind the question. Perhaps the questionner believed that if we educated Christians they would return to their homes better able to spread the gospel. I have thought about that and decided that if I wanted to spread the gospel of Jesus Christ to the young of the world, I would not want to talk only with those who were already Christian, but would chose to be with nonbelievers as well. I think my strategy might be to gather into a small group a few of the young from different ends of the earth, and to love them, and to care for them, to confirm their gifts, listen to their conflicts and disparate yearnings, and let them know that I am also a pilgrim on the earth in need of companions on the Way. If I succeeded, they might return to their homes and be able to say what Christianity was about, and I might become a universal person.

In a pamphlet entitled, *What is the Family of Man?* Pastor Ted Noffs of Australia writes:

> If one looks across the world today, one will discover that the greatest barrier to world peace is religion. The trouble spots across the globe that are most dangerous are from locations where there is religious enmity.
>
> How ironic it is that world religions which have often claimed to act in the name of an all loving God are the centrepoints of hatreds that have brought the world to the threshold of annihilation.
>
> This is the fundamental question facing mankind because upon the answer to this question rests the survival of humanity. For this reason, the removal of religious hatred, beginning with little children and proceeding right through to the adults in our society, is the most urgent task facing men and women of good will. Along with other world problems, we see religious hatred as one of the most challenging and formidable of social concerns threatening the survival of life on planet Earth.

Religious hatred is more subtle and not as discernible in the society in which those of us in the churches move. In our own way we call "profane" what God has made "clean." Peter's great insight is not deeply ours. "The truth I have now come to realize," he said "is that God does not have favorites, but that anybody of any nationality who fears God and does what is right is acceptable to him" (Acts 10:34–35 Jer.).

I remember when Conrad Hoover sent my book, *Search for Silence,* to a church group that was exploring with him the possibility of his leading a retreat. They cancelled the whole idea when they found Eastern mystics and men of unbelief represented in the anthology sections.

Prejudice is not a trait of the religious only. In secular circles I do not like to admit that I work for a church. Curtains come down all around and that is not good for self-esteem or dialogue. Prejudice is rampant in our society. Many of the unchurched have stamped "religious types" as belonging to an inferior race. The churched and the unchurched are usually looking at each other with feelings of superiority, each harboring in his soul the feeling of being the "enlightened one."

For my own journeying and encouragement I have held close the words of Saint Augustine, "Where I found truth, there found I my God," and those of another lonely seeker, Simone Weil, who wrote, "Christ likes us to prefer truth to him because, before being Christ, he is truth. If one turns aside for him to go toward the truth, one will not go far before falling into his arms."[9]

Martin Buber gives helpful guidance when he writes, "By no means. . .can it be our true task. . .to turn away from the things and beings that we meet on our way and that attract our hearts; our task is precisely to get in touch with them, by hallowing our relationship with them, with what manifests itself in them as beauty, pleasure, enjoyment. Hasidism teaches that rejoicing in the world, if we hallow it with our whole being, leads to rejoicing in God."[10]

The Scriptures give authority to the words of these friends. They say distinctly that things and beings which bear the name of "Christian" are not necessarily Christian, and one who calls himself an unbeliever might in reality be closer to God than the one who is full of boast about who he is. Jesus is always talking about the Kingdom of God belonging not to those who say the right words, but to those who yield the proper fruit. It is sobering to read:

> Not everyone who calls me "Lord, Lord" will enter the kingdom of Heaven, but only those who do the will of my heavenly Father. When that day comes, many will say to me, "Lord, Lord, did we not prophesy in your name, cast out devils in your name, and in your name perform many miracles?" Then I will tell them to their face, "I never knew you: out of my sight, you and your wicked ways!"
> (Matt. 7:21–23 NEB)

The whole spirit of Jesus implies that there is no one house of worship—neither there nor here—neither at our retreat center in the country nor at our chapel in the city, "neither on this mountain, nor in Jerusalem. . . . Those who are real worshippers will worship the Father in spirit and in truth" (John 4:21–23 NEB). Jesus is the Way, and he taught that the Way is justice, mercy and love, the Way is a passionate commitment to truth.

Thought, however, is safe, only for those whose sense of self is rooted in a transcendent God. R. V. Sampson points out that when this is not so a person is "very prone to derive his sense of significance from the values of the group or groups with which he identifies himself. Accordingly any threat to those groups will be experienced as a threat to the stability of the individual ego identifying with them."[11] To be intellectually alive means to be in pursuit of more than classroom learning. It is to lean one's elbow upon one's own knee, to cup one's head in one's own hand, and to think.

Let us remember, however, as we make our commitment to be servants of the truth wherever we find it, or wherever it is uncovered for us, that religion developed on the intellectual side alone is cold and dogmatic, full of doctrine, argument and endless discussion. The reality is that we always know so little of what is to be known. When we have faced all the facts, checked our calculations and put our statistical tables in order, we are not knowledgeable. We still have not measured the heights of the sky or plumbed the depths of the abyss. If you will recall, the Genesis story says that the sin in the Garden was our desire to have knowledge of good and of evil—of what is right and of what is wrong.

> One alone is wise, the Lord most terrible seated upon his throne
> (Eccles. 1:8 NEB).

An important bit of knowledge is that he gives each one a measure of his wisdom, and in plenty to those who love him. One other thing about the knowledge that God gives is that it never puffs up. God gives this wisdom in order that we may discern our secret faults. Knowing the truth about ourselves makes us humble and open to truth in the world.

*Elizabeth*

## NOTES

1. Alan Moorehead, *Darwin and The Beagle* (New York: Harper & Row, Publishers, Inc., 1969).
2. Moorehead, *Darwin*, pp. 30–31.
3. Moorehead, *Darwin*, p. 31.
4. (New York: Doubleday & Company, Inc., 1958), p. 194.
5. Eiseley, *Darwin's Century*, p. 198.
6. Ibid., pp. 351–352.
7. Sigmund Freud & Oskar Pfister, *Psychoanalysis and Faith* (New York: Basic Books, Inc., 1963), p. 63.
8. Robert Coles, *Erik H. Erikson, the Growth of His Work* (Boston, Toronto: Little, Brown and Company, 1970), pp. 198–99.
9. Simone Weil, *Waiting for God* (New York: Harper & Row, Publishers, Inc., 1973), p. 69.
10. Martin Buber, *The Way of Man* (London: Rouledge & Kegan Paul, 1950), p. 20.
11. R. V. Sampson, *The Psychology of Power* (New York: Pantheon Books, 1966), p. 204.

# 9

# *ON* OUR
# EMOTIONAL
# CENTER

*Dear Brothers and Sisters:*

The third dimension of our lives that needs attention is the emotional. This center will be arrested in its development unless it is informed by the historical and intellectual. Each center needs the input of the others. At the same time each center needs to be nurtured in its individual growth, if there is to be a reciprocal dialogue between them.

To be mature in the area of the emotional is to be in touch with our feelings and to learn to be sincere about them. What does it mean then to be sincere about feelings? The dictionary defines sincerity as pure, unadulterated, honest, free from hypocrisy. The obsolete definition is "whole; uninjured." How strange that this latter definition which rings so true should have passed out of common understanding. The person who is sincere about his feelings generally has a sense of well-being.

I know that I feel health in myself when my words do not betray my heart. I may sometimes be anxious because I am not certain I will be received when my feelings and thoughts are not the popular ones, but I am able to cope with the burden of that fear when I consider the place of sincerity in any trek toward wholeness.

When we are emotionally honest we do not pretend to feelings that we do not have. This becomes extraordinarily difficult for us all when we are dealing with negative and aggressive feelings in ourselves and others. It is not common emotional knowledge that all human beings have ambivalent feelings. Simultaneously we are drawn toward and repulsed from an object, person or action. We know this with our heads, but our hearts do not allow for it.

We are too busy shielding ourselves from negative emotions to enter into dialogue with them or about them. The kingdom within does not grow peaceful. The lamb and the lion who dwell there do not lie down together. The opposites in us are never reconciled because we are not able to work with what we do not acknowledge. This ill prepares us for the work of reconciliation in the world.

Love in families and then in new communities is usually incomplete because we have no understanding that wholeness is dependent on an engagement with negative feelings. The popular conception is that the negative must be eliminated rather than treated as a givenness that is part of our life. Our negative feelings may have the precious function of driving us toward holiness. Always a new dimension of the lion and the lamb will emerge. Always we will have the task of harmonizing the polarities.

For example, anger helps us to know that we have been hurt or that others have been hurt. It helps us to set things right for ourselves and to make a new thrust toward love. Envy, if we catch its message, will help us to move toward praise. It is the emotion that goads us to discover vocation, pointing us toward the development and use of our gifts. A person doing what she or he was born to do is seldom envious. In the same way, other emotions surface to give us the information that we need, if we are to choose life.

The difficulty is that we have been taught to fear our feelings —especially the negative ones. We are afraid of negativity in others and tremble before any expression of our own. We shrink from letting others know when they offend our sense of justice or violate our sensitivities, or make us feel that we are misused—all of which takes place in any community. The fact that we are lopsided in the development of our different centers means that our values will be different, and that we will come at things in different ways. It means that we will have difficulty making ourselves clear. We will call the same things by different names, viewing the same facts but coming to different conclusions. We will misunderstand and be misunderstood, and find anger and resentment rising in us. After all, the other person "should know better."

So it is that one of the primary issues facing any people is the handling of negative feelings. If a community fails to provide structures for dialogue and the honest expression of one's self, the integrity of the community will suffer, and members will remain at immature levels of emotional development.

The communities which provide the greatest opportunity and space for the handling of differences seem to be those whose members live together on some day-to-day basis. Perhaps the sheer necessity of survival pushes the matter to the top of agendas. Even those communities are sometimes slow to move toward the real questions of shared life, and are often more likely to focus on shared economics rather than on shared feelings.

Now and then we are even afraid to let our simple wishes be made known. In a recent gathering of members we were giving illustrations of how we fail to work with our negative responses. One person said that in his office a co-worker kept the music system going all the time. When she was absent it was turned off, but on her return she would invariably put it back on. Although many felt resentment, no one was willing to face the sharp response that any objection to the music would inevitably provoke. Finally one person mustered sufficient courage to turn the music off. She was pointedly ignored for two weeks by the affronted one. In that office, the issue is still being skirted. Disagreeable situations are too often handled in this manner. We think if we do nothing about them that they will go away. In actuality we cannot step over a problem without paying a price. The larger the problem, the larger the cost. Not even the child is exempt from the consequence of avoidance. This particular example is also illustrative of how a group will allow one person to dominate a situation.

Another member related how she had made a small house available to her mother and a companion. They then invited a friend to live in the house with them, which infuriated the daughter, who now felt that she was supporting three people. "I am churning inside," she said, "but I would rather churn than bring it up with them."

There are as many variations to these scenarios as there are persons. They account for the popularity of courses in "assertiveness training," and books with titles like *Taking Care of Myself*. These offerings are sometimes derided as indulgence in self-centeredness, which may be too simple a reading. I am quite convinced that the church is the community of those who derive meaning from living for others, but we make a tragic mistake if we try to move toward that lifestyle by being dishonest about what we are feeling. This wreaks havoc with our emotional integrity and gives piety a bad name. We have also equated caring for others with not caring for ourselves, thus pushing ourselves into roles of dependency. After all, if I cannot look out for myself, I must find someone to look out for me and, as dependent people discover, this is a full-time occupation that leaves very little time to care for anyone else, and certainly does not make for emotional maturity.

In a world where honesty of expression is not practiced, we cannot trust the nice things we hear about ourselves. As for the bad things we are told, they devastate us, or make us defensive or angry. We are all very fragile, but the opposite is also true—we are tougher than we think. In therapy groups where the injunction is to struggle with expressing one's feelings, again and again participants have the experience of saying to someone in the group, "What you said makes me angry," and, a few minutes later, of saying to that same person, "I want you to know that I no longer feel resentful toward you." The stating of one's feelings can change those feelings, even without the dialogue that always ensues. Unlike the priest and the psychiatrist we do not give ourselves the opportunity to know this. We tend to think that when a person is saying how things are between him and another it is going to be that way forever. We all know with our heads that this is not the case, but the heart has other experiences, and is slow to understand that the anger that is expressed and heard does not become a "root of bitterness."

The deeper the wound, the greater the outrage, and the more times the story will have to be told for healing to occur. This is not to say that all hurt feelings are justified or all outrage real, but one discovers one's own responsibility in an atmosphere where there is freedom to express unreasonable as well as reasonable complaints. Indeed, which of us is wise enough to know the difference in advance of speaking? The wise man of Ecclesiasticus says:

> A reproof may be untimely,
> and silence may show a man's good sense.
> Yet how much better it is to complain than to nurse a
> grudge, and confession saves a man from disgrace.
>
> (Ecclus. 20:1–2 NEB)

Ecclesiasticus had more help to give than this:

> Do not find fault before examining the evidence;
> think first, and criticize afterwards.
> Do not answer without first listening,
> and do not interrupt when another is speaking.
>
> (Ecclus. 11:7–9 NEB)

We need these and other guidelines if we are to become healers of one another, able to endure the confessions that each of us has to make. Certainly within our own small communities we must have a lasting commitment to one another, so that each knows that the other is not going to pull out of the relationship when the going gets rough.

Small therapy groups require each person to make a commitment not to leave a group until he has met with the group twice to discuss the reason of his withdrawing. The covenant recognizes the temptation to run away when we have heard things we do not want to hear, or our community does not respond with the sensitivity to which we think we are entitled, or we are threatened by our own feelings or thoughts. After all, rocking boats sink and shaking foundations bring houses down.

The covenant that checks our flight also creates a climate of safety for all the members who know that if they goof things up, offend or hurt others, there is "another chance." The fear of permanent rejection is the chief of all our fears and the one which keeps us from being honest about who we are. We want to be accepted, approved and liked, sometimes even by the people whom we do not accept, or approve or like. The human heart shrinks from the pain of rejection. We fear being "left out," or not "fitting in." We find ourselves incapable of enduring large rejction, though many of us would say that we have recovered from the times when it did happen to us, if indeed we remember those times at all. Our fear may be ample evidence, however, that once upon a time it did take place and that in the psyche where nothing is ever lost the pain was duly recorded.

In a world grounded in love, and in human beings created to give and to receive love, it is no small wonder that the greatest suffering is rooted in rejection and the fear of abandonment. God gave us free will, but he also made it extraordinarily difficult for us not to choose the way of relationship and of love. Every time we do not make that choice our life becomes more narrow and restricted. He chose us and made a world in which we suffer when we do not choose each other. We prate about free choice, but how much choice is there in a system so rigged for love?

We do terrible things to each other and to ourselves, because we have not learned to be in tune with our own nature, to know what we think, feel and want. We all come into adulthood wounded, which for the most part means that we have been rejected, or have failed to hear the messages sounding through our own beings, or have chosen that with which we are not comfortable. What we have come to know is that the origin of most of our troubles is childhood—those helpless, dependent infant years.

In her recent book, which every adult should rush to read, Selma Fraiberg writes:

> During the first six months, the baby has the rudiments of a love language available to him. There is the language of the embrace, the language of the eyes, the language of the smile, vocal communications of pleasure and distress. It is the essential vocabulary of love before we can speak of love. Eighteen years later, when the baby is full grown and "falls in love" for the first time, he will woo his partner through the utterance of endearments, and the joy of the

embrace. In his declarations of love he will use such phrases as "When I first looked into your eyes," "When you smiled at me," "When I held you in my arms," and naturally, in his exalted state, he will believe that he invented this love song.[1]

While Dr. Fraiberg points out that the baby's rudimentary love language belongs to an innate repertoire, she also points out that love is the gift that parents give:

> We now know that those qualities that we call "human"—the capacity for enduring love and the exercise of conscience—are not given in human biology; they are the achievement of the earliest human partnership, that between a child and his parents.
> And we now know that a child who is deprived of human partners in the early years of life, or has known shifting or unstable partnerships in the formative period of personality, may suffer permanent impairment in his capacity to love, to learn, to judge, and to abide by the laws of the human community. This child, in effect, has been deprived of his humanity.[2]

In increasing numbers today's children are growing up without the gift-giving, gift-evoking mother and father. They are the children of the slums, the children of working mothers, of teenagers, of depressed and anxious mothers who are, for all intents and purposes, absent mothers. In my own middle-class circles they are the children of ambitious parents, whose standards their children can never quite meet. Throughout their lives, beneath the surface of all they attempt and accomplish, these so-called "privileged children" hear the gentle, goading voice of a father or a mother suggesting, "If only you tried, you could do better." With such "wonderful" parents they have a hard time understanding why they are cloaked in the feeling of never measuring up.

Our inability to handle the anger and resentment generated by small and large grievances is the basis of failure in child-parent relationships, as it is the basis of failures in so many marriages and friendships. Even two people with a commitment to spend their lives with each other may let their unspoken thoughts and feelings become a solid wall between them, a dividing wall of hostility. Almost any two can get by with this for a few years but, by the time fifteen years have gone by in a relationship, the stockpiled feelings—anger, wishes, hopes and resentments—are so high that the two can no longer see each other over the top of them.

In penetrating, frightening words, Tillie Olsen, in the opening paragraph of her story, *Tell Me a Riddle*,[3] describes what happens in one way or another for too many of us:

> For forty-seven years they had been married. How deep back the stubborn gnarled roots of the quarrel reached, no one could say— but only now, when tending to the needs of others no longer shackled them together, the roots swelled up visible, split the earth between them, and the tearing shook even to the children, long since grown.

It is as hard to express positive thoughts as negative ones. We take it for granted that the other will not guess our critical appraisal, but somehow we expect the other to divine when we are feeling appreciative, or admiring, or simply turning gentle thoughts in our hearts. The stark fact is that we are scared to death to talk to each other.

What difference does it make if we have with our minds produced the technology that enables us to pick up the telephone and speak to any person any place in the world, when we do not know how to talk heart to heart with the people in our own households? We have the resources to feed the hungry, but the eyes of our hearts do not see them. We who might be the beneficiaries of technology are its victims. The real energy that will enable the creations of our minds and hands to serve us is dependent on a developed emotional life.

Our own New Land communities are almost three years old. We can still see above the stockpile of our unspoken hopes, wishes and resentments, the secret and not so secret grievances that we nurse. Fifteen, even five years from now, that will no longer be true. Ephesians says, ". . .Do not let the sun go down on your anger" (Eph. 4:26 RSV). Will those who struggle to build the community called Church take with seriousness even that one sentence of Scripture? Can we commit ourselves to working for structures that make it easier for persons to share themselves?

We have not learned to relate to each other in deep and

nourishing ways and for that each of us must pay a fierce price. The Christian community, however, understands lost relationships and our cries for help, or it would not have a cross at its heart. We are the community of the Cross as well as the community of the Resurrection. If we forget either one of these realities we will be incapable of struggling for the truth of Christianity. Yes, we are the community of joy and celebration, but neither joy nor celebration exist apart from our complicated and anguished lives.

Experience in Christian community is always made up of deaths, burials and fresh beginnings. How else can a people rise on behalf of a world that does not know the message of its unity? There is little community or communion in the world because we have so little understanding of what is required of each of us to deal with our own false perceptions of how things are with us. Christian community grows out of repentance, which means facing the truth about ourselves.

But how many people seeking Christian community are saying, "I want to know the truth about myself"? Instead, they cling to their idealized pictures of what community should be. More than this, they want this community overnight, and when it fails to meet their needs, they begin to ask, "What is wrong with us?" or more likely, "What is wrong with them?"

In my own community there is always someone to suggest that we have more meetings and someone to suggest that we have fewer, and as many variations on that theme as we have people. Of course, we do not hear each other because we are each speaking from a different center. That alone produces a babble of tongues. Adding to the confusion of outer conflicts are our respective inner conflicts. Our head tells us one thing, and our feelings another, and the two are not in correspondence. They do not listen to each other any more than the kingdoms of the world listen to each other.

Only in the heart does every word of Scripture have a literal translation. While the head raises a question or argues a point, the heart puts forth its demand for a Garden event. It knows about imprisonment and slavery, burning bushes, the cry for deliverance, Red Seas and deserts, prophets and angels, the promised Messiah. The lonely, forsaken, crushed heart with the cry, "Come Lord Jesus, come," knows all the details about a flood and an ark for which Darwin was searching. It knows about descending doves, desertion, trial, death, community and communion. Woe to us if we do not give the emotional dimension of our lives proper attention, if we fail to take care of these foolish hearts of ours. They are the place of our meeting with God. Baron von Hügel wisely pairs the mystical with the emotional, as he equates the institutional with the historical and the scientific with the intellectual.

While Scripture speaks of a transcendent order, it recognizes the unity between the inner life and the outer life, and says unquestionably that our meeting with God is determined by the nature of our meeting with each other. If I am aware that you have something against me, and I have not been to see you and tried to understand my role in your grievance, then I cannot be close to the Father. Our relationship with others is always a mirror of our relationship with God. What we hide from others we end up hiding from ourselves. The call upon us is to be incredibly and staggeringly open with each other. Community happens when we dare to be naked not only in the presence of God but in the presence of each other, dare to let others see our weaknesses and our strengths, dare to let another hold us accountable.

Our culture has honored the intellect and denigrated feelings. Now in the process of righting the imbalance, we hear much more about the emotional life. The fears that biased us in favor of the intellect are not unfounded. Every age has its terrible examples of persons and groups ruled by emotions alone. Witch hunts, lynchings, heresies, the Nazi cry, "Think with your blood," is history we cannot afford to forget. Even when emotions are not evil, without the intellect they lack power. So Paul was prompted to write: "Anybody who has the gift of tongues must pray for the power of interpreting them. For if I use this gift in my prayers, my spirit may be praying but my mind is left barren. What is the answer to that? Surely I should pray not only with the spirit but with the mind as well? And sing praises not only with the spirit but with the mind as well" (1 Cor. 14:13–16 Jer.).

The struggle of the women's movement is a struggle to develop the gift of intellect, which can be fully developed only if it is fully used. Women are no longer willing to live out the emotional side for men, or to allow men to live out the intellectual side for them. They are insisting that the imbalance be corrected. They are not only claiming the fact that they are persons of intellect, but demanding the right to use that intellect in the affairs of the world.

Men, in numbers large enough to be noticeable, have begun to use unashamedly a full range of emotions. They are claiming their right to tears, embraces and tender feelings, and to stay home—to cook and sew and care for children. One day they may even admit the feeling of being afraid to be murdered in war. Some of them have already been willing to pay the price of refusing to go to war.

I think also of the women who were willing to be the clowns of history marching down Fifth Avenue with their ridiculous banners claiming the vote for women. I have for them the same gratitude that I feel for those in this decade who have insisted on their own Garden story. If sometimes their voices seemed a bit shrill, and their words angry and exaggerated, it is small wonder. Not many were friendly to their thoughts, and there were so few of them to do the work for so many of us.

The real issue between men and women today is the development of the whole person. The way men and women relate to one another is changing and will continue to change as each develops forgotten or neglected dimensions in themselves. We are moving toward a time when men and women can be fully themselves with each other, and be friends even when they are not lovers. Many of the young have made strides in this direction, but each of us has a work to do to hasten that day which promises to hold a deeper communion. Along the way will be obstacles to overcome as there are obstacles along every path to liberation. But what else can we do? We cannot return to innocence. Once more in our history is a Garden, a gate, the cherubim and flashing swords.

While there is peril in not developing each of the centers I have been writing about in my letters to you, the danger is diminished by the recognition of the work we all must do. If we can awake to our own undeveloped sides, we will be more open to seeking the information that we need to make mature decisions and to resolve conflicts between persons and nations.

Christianity talks about our growing up into the mature stature of Christ and of pressing toward the goal. But Christianity also talks about a journey along the path of which we are to bear the burdens of each other's undeveloped side. If we are aware that despite our best efforts we may not get it all together, we will look to others for what we lack in ourselves.

When Charles Darwin left Her Majesty's ship, The Beagle, he was destined to grow in his lopsidedness, so captured was his mind by the questions he had begun to ask. His wife never tried to divert him from his studies, but was content to be with him in his lopsidedness. He in his turn was accepting of her though she had no interest in the things that engaged him. His biographer wrote, "Once when they attended a scientific lecture together he said to her, 'I am afraid this is very wearisome to you.' 'Not more than all the rest,' she said."[4] He might have been angered by such a reply, but instead he enjoyed quoting it. Nonetheless, Darwin felt the impoverishment of living so fully out of the intellectual/scientific dimension of his life. As an old man he wrote in his journal, "I wish that I had found time to read a poem each day."

Though not many of us have Darwin's genius, we must all the same allow each other our lopsidedness. I know that I make small headway against the imbalance in myself. I think that I shall be forever caught by studies of the human heart. Though I know as well as you that it cannot be dissected, or catalogued, or predicted, something tells me that it has secrets that can be known. If I do not press my interests on you too often, perhaps you will be tolerant of me when I do. I, in turn, will forgive you your concentrations. It may be that we are each like one part of a mosaic window. We transmit only a portion of light and a part of the picture. We have no particular beauty in ourselves, but when we are fitted into the pattern which includes us all, the light of Christ will break on the world. Is this not what Paul was saying when he told the Corinthians that "God put all the separate parts into the body on purpose. If all the parts were the same, how could it be a body?" (1 Cor. 12:18–20 Jer.).

Because of our drives as well as our hidden and obvious

handicaps, we may not be able to develop equally in all the dimensions of our lives. When we understand and accept this, we are in a position to receive from the other what we need for a balanced view of the world. That humble state also makes it possible for others to call forth long buried parts of our natures.

Perhaps the Kingdom person—the servant leader—is the one who has achieved equal development in all his or her dimensions, and is thus able to reconcile within his or her own being the differences in us and between us. We are not all at that point, but we all have that vocation—to understand, to accept, to forgive and to encourage one another in the upward calling of God in Christ.

*Elizabeth*

P.S. I would recommend as a group exercise that each person identify the dimension in which he or she feels most developed —emotional, intellectual, or historical. Indicate the activities you enjoy that confirm this. What dimension have you most neglected? What do you feel would nurture your growth in this area? Check out your perceptions with group members.

### NOTES

1. *Every Child's Birthright* (New York: Basic Books, Inc., 1978), p. 29.
2. *Every Child's Birthright,* p. 113.
3. *Tell Me a Riddle* (Philadelphia and New York: J. B. Lippincott, 1961), p. 93.
4. Moorehead, *Darwin and The Beagle,* p. 249.

# 10

# *ON* OUR MOVING CENTER

## *Dear Sisters and Brothers:*

While underscoring von Hügel's caution to maintain a creative tension among the emotional, intellectual and historical elements of religion, I found myself wanting to give an equal place to the moving center in each of us, which also must be nurtured for a "full and fruitful religion." There are, of course, other centers too, but if we neglect the moving dimension of our lives, our focus on other centers will be useless. Every inward work requires an outward expression, or it comes to nought. In fact, it may even fracture us further, widening the split between what we inwardly subscribe to and what we outwardly do. This is why a person's work is always of utmost importance. "Being" and "doing" complete each other, as do "staying" and "going." We cannot choose one above the other without falling into great trouble. Kenneth Patchen, the poet, wrote:[1]

> Isn't all our dread a dread of being
> Just here? Of being only this?
> Of having no other thing to become?
> Of having nowhere to go really
> But where we are?

The moving center carries us out into the world. This center holds the Abraham in us, the one who is always seeking the New Land. This center is more conscious of the Christ who waits "outside the gate" (Heb. 13:13 Jer.) than of the Christ who is Emmanuel, "God with us." The moving center looks toward the future and asks the question, "What must I do to hasten the coming of Christ?"

According to the biblical perspective, wave after wave of goodness, beauty and love are beating against the doors to consciousness, and will break them down. The question is do we really understand life this way? Do we feel that there is a whole new world seeking to come into being, or do we experience life as essentially moving toward death? Are the problems that confront us of such magnitude that no one knows what to do? Is it a matter of holding on until the cities of the world explode or crumble back into the dark ages, or do we through the Risen Christ and his presence in us, sense that God might use the womb of our lives to bring something completely unexpected into the world?

If we are, indeed, to be the harbinger of the new, we must give attention to the moving center. This is the center which carries us out into the world to be the builders of a new heaven and a new earth. Like the other centers, it does not function well unless it is recognized, challenged and supported. In a sermon, Gordon Cosby suggested that we might do this by using the image of the bud found in the Scripture:

> Here and now I will do a new thing; this moment it will break from the bud. Can you not perceive it?        (Isa. 43:18 NEB)

Gordon indicated that we could each work with the passage from Isaiah by giving attention to naming the bud in ourselves that was seeking to break forth. After doing this exercise in my small mission group, I would recommend it to you. What is the area that is pregnant within the world? And pregnant within your faith community, but most important, pregnant within yourself? So much of the time we rush into action without identifying the new thing that God is trying to do through us. Like Darwin's trying to be a doctor, our efforts are expended in one thing while our energy seeks to flow in another direction. We can discover the new that God is trying to do through us only by checking within to see where all the sap is building up. That is where the bud is, where God is pushing us out. Within each of us is such a place. "Keep looking," said Gordon, "until you find it, and then write down what you see." These are the same instructions that Habakkuk gave:

> Write the vision down, inscribe it on tablets to be easily read, since this vision is for its own time only: eager for its own fulfilment, it does not deceive                                 (Hab. 2:2–3 Jer.)

Obviously Habakkuk was a strong advocate of journal keeping. Even in a time when crude methods of inscription made the assignment difficult, he urged the writing down of visions. He knew that, in the same way that buds want to flower, visions want to be fulfilled, or they dry up and make for cynicism or bitterness.

Another evident characteristic of Habakkuk is his immense confidence in each person's capacity to have a vision. He said,

> If it comes slowly, wait, for come it will, without fail.
>                                      (Hab. 2:3 Jer.)

We need those words of encouragement. For some of us images will be slow to form. We have not exercised our capacity to imagine, nor have we even thought that we could have mental images of something not yet present. Under Habakkuk's tutelage one's imagination would not have atrophied. Said this prophet:

> I will stand on my watchtower, and take up my post on my battlements, watching to see what he will say to me, what answer he will make to my complaints.                         (Hab. 2:1 Jer.)

The prophet had his own troubles. Despite them, or because of them, he had learned some secrets of a deep spirituality. It would not occur to many of us to stand back from our own lives, observe the battles within us, cry out our grievances and then watch for the images floating across the screens of our minds.

People constantly complain about what is happening in the world and what is happening to them. We are acute observers of the clash between good and evil, but we have no sense of ourselves as instruments of God's justice. We are much more apt to feel that we are the victims—that things are out of our hands. The seats of power are too far removed from us. What is there to do about terrorists on the streets except to bar windows, and about terrorists in the skies, except to increase the security system. We do not know God as the Holy One who never dies, and his church as the people "watching to see what he will say. . . ."

If we do have a vision, we are apt to discount it by saying that we have been on a "fantasy trip" or have been "wool gathering."

Ours is not the only generation that has neglected watching or whose imaginations are frozen. In 1 Samuel it is written, "It was rare for Yahweh to speak in those days; visions were uncommon" (3:1 Jer.). Three times God called to Samuel without his knowing that it was God calling. Each time he ran to Eli saying, "Here I am, since you called me." The third time Eli understood that it was Yahweh who was calling the boy, and told him:

> "Go and lie down, and if someone calls say, 'Speak, Yahweh, your servant is listening.'" So Samuel went and lay down in his place.
>
> (1 Sam. 3:9 Jer.)
>
> The next time God called to him, Samuel answered: "Speak, Yahweh, your servant is listening."
>
> (1 Sam. 3:10 Jer.)

Only then does God give Samuel a vision of a better world, and how it is to be brought about. I have turned to these Scriptures for the help that they give us in the discernment of call. They seem to say very clearly that we are to watch and we are to listen. The theme is repeated many times and in many ways in the New Testament. "Have you *eyes that do not see, ears that do not hear*?" (Mark 8:18 Jer.).

In biblical accounts, a mark of conversion is an openness to the reality of God's address in people, events and things. When our hearts have been changed we discern in ordinary happenings and words the direction in which we are to go, and find continuing confirmation of our election.

Part of our difficulty in moving out after we have perceived the bud is that we lack confidence. We do not believe that we can bring about what we see. Low self-esteem, a raging disease in the world today, invades every area of our lives. Even those who dare to see visions and have dreams do not engage in any action that would bring them to fulfillment. Initially, biblical people seem to suffer from the same lack of confidence. They, too, saw visions, heard God's call, and declared themselves unfit for what he had in mind for them to do.

Moses says,

> "Who am I to go to Pharaoh and bring the sons of Israel out of Egypt?"                                     (Exod. 3:11–12 Jer.)

Saul, although often accused of ambition, is no more eager.

> "Am I not a Benjaminite, from the smallest of Israel's tribes? And is not my family the least of all the families of the tribe of Benjamin? Why do you say such words to me?"          (1 Sam. 9:21 Jer.)

Jeremiah succumbs to feelings of helplessness.

> "Ah, Lord Yahweh; look, I do not know how to speak: I am a child!"                                     (Jer. 1:6 Jer.)

What caused the change that happened in these folk of long ago? If we knew, perhaps we would find help for our own sinking hearts, and the buds in us would have some chance of coming to flower. In one breath the biblical leaders say, "I am not adequate; find someone else," and in the next "Here I am, send me" (Isa. 6:9 Jer.). In each case the shift in feeling seems to carry with it the recognition that they will not be traveling alone. There is One who will go with them. "Do not be afraid. I am with you to protect you. . ." (Jer. 1:8 Jer.). They know themselves to be in the service of God, "singled out," as it were.

What change must take place in us if we are to have that same experience? My own feeling is that we have to come to grips with the fact that the inadequacy that we feel is in one sense an accurate evaluation of the situation. That feeling of helplessness, or frustration, or fear that arises from the pit of the stomach when confronting any large task is not necessarily a neurosis making us turn back. It may be a healthy warning signal. Unless some mysterious synthesis takes place most of us are not able to fulfill the visions and the dreams that are given to us.

If we think that we have only ourselves to rely on, we will never get started. We have to throw in our widow's mite, move out in trust and know that what we lack will be supplied. We have to be radically obedient to the vision that has been given to us, saying, "Here I am, send me." God's Spirit descends on such a person. His heart is changed, his fears dispelled. As his energy begins to flow, enthusiasm is generated. Other people are drawn and contribute their gifts. Signs are given and, in time, the new bursts forth out of the womb of one's own life.

As a writer, working with individual call, this has also been my experience. I see the bud. I have a vision of a work that might be healing, but I have no sense that I can bring it to completion. Also, somewhere along the way I begin to doubt the worth of what I want to say. After all, nothing is new under the sun. It has all been said before. And anyway, who am I to presume that others want me to share with them my heart and mind? Usually by sheer will power I overcome the enormous resistances in myself to begin a piece of writing. After that things fall into place. Thoughts are given, words flow and somewhere out of my sight a work of organization goes on. This does not mean that I do not still have an arduous piece of writing to do. Always I must keep throwing in my widow's mite.

This has to be true of the *new* that *anyone* is called to do. If the new work is not yet present, and therefore cannot be copied, or repeated, or reproduced, extraordinary effort is required.

What is true for an individual call is true for the corporate call. Recently Janelle Goetcheus, a member of The Church of the Saviour, wanted to bring into being a city health center with a number of medical and counseling services. Janelle is a medical doctor, who with her husband and children moved to the Washington area so that she might nurture her vision of working with the poor. The more she moved out on her vision, the more it unfolded until she reached a time of readiness in her spirit and issued her own call for the creation of structures that would have the potential of bringing a whole new quality of health care to inner city residents. She had no sooner announced her commitment to the vision than people essential to the new ministry came to join with her.

One was Karen Michaelson, who, quite independently, had developed her concept of a ministry to the total person. The other was Chas Griffin, a therapist and old friend who was living in Buffalo, New York. Though he had an extensive practice he was aware of feelings of envy when his friend shared with him what she was doing in Washington. When she called with her news of the health center it was like a gong sounding the time in him. "I am coming," he said.

Another friend offered help in securing funds, and a manufacturing company in the West made a gift of four examining tables. Of course, none of this is as easy as it might sound in the telling. When the vision is still a vision how do you gracefully furnish your house with four examining tables and not feel crowded? How do you uproot yourself and family and not do battle with demons and angels?

"Here I am, send me," is a reply that is full of agony and ecstasy. Such is the story of every mission that has come into being since The Church of the Saviour community was born 30 years ago, and is probably the story since time began.

If we are not changed by experiences like these, the reason may be a dearth of reflection in our individual and corporate lives. We petition God for his direction and help, but we do not reflect enough on our days to realize when they are given. We are inclined to think that what was accomplished was all of our own doing—the letter we wrote, the telephone call we made, the excellent promotion material that we used, each of which was essential, but all of which, taken together, would have been insufficient. Infused by the Spirit, a confidence came that evoked confidence, a trust that inspired others to put aside cautious ways, a lilt to the voice that brought tidings of good things to come. In reflection we will know that Another came and added himself to the company of the called.

The New Testament has other prototypes to overcome the self-doubts that flood us when we think about fulfilling our visions. One is Mary, who describes herself as a "lowly hand-maid," who sings the Magnificat:

> Yes, from this day forward all generations will call me blessed, for the Almighty has done great things for me. (Luke 1:48–49 Jer.)

Small wonder that God chose Mary to be the mother of Jesus. How many of us would be humble and confident enough to know that what is stirring in us is of God, and to sing the Magnificat. This week a friend said to me, "In my household we were supposed to work very hard, but not hard enough to succeed, because that might lead to hubris. And yet," he said, "I cannot feel that my schemes are grandiose. I feel that God has something grand for me to do."

Each of us has the vocation to be as whole a person as Mary was. Each of us has the vocation to be a bearer of God's word. Each of us has something grand to do. This is my understanding of Scripture. It does not even matter that we are a bit neurotic—even very neurotic. Who are we to complain about God's handiwork? Neither the prophets nor the disciples are presented as men who are mature in mind and heart. We are to move out in confidence. God, in keeping with his nature, did a God-like thing; he so made us that we can use even our neurotic symptoms and conflicts for creative and constructive work and, more amazing yet, in the process be healed. This is the message that Erik Erikson, the psychoanalyst, gives us in his studies of Ghandi and the young man Luther. This may be the message bequeathed us in Isaiah's words:

> Cease to dwell on days gone by and to brood over past history.
> (Isa. 43:18 NEB)

The future will not be a repetition of the past. It does not matter how damaged our lives are or what forces for destruction are loose in the world, God is going to do something which is totally new.

> Now I show you new things, hidden things which you did not know before. They were not created long ago, but in this very hour; you had never heard of them before today. You cannot say, "I know them already." (Isa. 48:6–7 NEB)

The new life throbbing within is not subject to being dragged back into the darkness. It is no longer life toward death, but life out of death. It is the earthly and visible presence of God in the world.

Mary is a prototype for us, but so is her son in our struggle to respond to call, as he is at the point of every other struggle for the supremacy of God in our lives. His society also had an emphasis on what money can buy and hard work achieve. If he had a vision of God's Kingdom, he also had a vision of power and glory, or there would be no temptation story. In Scripture it is written that he knew what was in men, and the reason? He knew what was in himself. Of the temptation story, Stephen Verney wrote:

> ...He knew the interlocking of good and evil within himself—the story of his adult life begins with his baptism, when the Spirit descends on him and he hears a voice from heaven saying, "Thou art my Son, my Beloved; on thee my favour rests." And immediately the Spirit drove him out into the desert, and there he remained for forty days tempted by Satan. He was among the wild beasts; and the angels waited on him. There could be no more dramatic words to express the tensions between good and evil. The same divine love drives him into the desert to become aware of his fleshly appetites, his worldly desire for power, and his satanic lust for spiritual pre-eminence. The wild beasts and the angels are not merely around him. The beasts roar within his own soul, and the angels open within him new dimensions of truth and understanding.[2]

It is not enough to see visions and dream dreams. We have to take them with enough seriousness to think about saying, "Here I am. Send me." Any consideration of that declaration will put us in the company of beasts and angels. We will have to confront not only the matter of our inadequacy; but also the choices to be made. Tending our moving center—the little bud growing in us—requires at the very least some reallocation of time and energy and money.

The grander the vision, the larger the cost. A very grand vision can cost us job and security, perhaps even home and friends. No wonder that we turn from the company of angels, dismissing our dreams as impractical, or having come too late in life. For its fulfillment our vision might require going to another city, or going back to school, or changing our field of work.

A change is difficult at 30, highly risky at 40, and pure folly at 50. At 30 persons are supposed to have found themselves, and to know the requirements for climbing a very predictable ladder. The facts that inner growth helps us to identify different buds, and that new life cycles push us into different areas of ourselves that cry for fulfillment are given little attention by personnel directors. They are more inclined to award the plodding, dependable and efficient, who can be counted on not to disturb the sleeping artist, revolutionary, or dreamer within themselves—those who never hear the cry, "Awake, O sleeper!" They too made a choice, and pay a fearful price. How can we begrudge them their rewards? They represent those of us who never do battle with beasts or angels because we have fallen asleep in life.

Ah, fateful vision, could it be that if I found myself in your service, I would be in the service of the Holy, become myself a holy person? I have the distinct feeling that this is the way holiness occurs. In the commitment of The Church of the Saviour is a line, "I unreservedly and with abandon commit my life and destiny to Christ." Surely in the area of action surrender means submission to a vision, a willingness to relinquish all that one holds dear in order to be faithful to what is seen only with the mind's eye. When we have faced our limitations, fidelity depends on the conviction that God will do his part. And there's the rub, for how trustworthy is God? Our intellectual center declares that it is his world, and that he will bring it to completion. The battle has been won in Jesus Christ. "I have a plan to carry out, and carry it out I will" (Isa. 46:11 NEB). We can participate, but fulfillment of the plan is not dependent on us. We are only half-convinced that we should presume to call ourselves co-creators, which implies equality in the effort. Our emotions, however, holding the reigns on our moving center, are giving an entirely different message, so that in actuality we act as though all depends on us, and as though God cannot be counted on to make any significant contribution, let alone hold up his side as co-creator. A pictorial view of all this is laid before us in Soren Kierkegaard's story of *The Domestic Goose:*

Suppose it were a fact that geese could talk. They then would have so arranged it that they could have their religious worship, their divine service. Every Sunday they came together, and a gander preached. The essential content of the sermon was: what a lofty destiny the goose had, what a high goal the Creator (and every time his name was mentioned the geese curtsied and the ganders bowed their heads) had set before the goose; by the aid of wings it could fly away to distant regions, blessed climes, where properly it was at home, for it was only a stranger here. So it was every Sunday. And as soon as the assembly broke up each waddled home to his own affairs. And again the next Sunday to divine worship, and then again home—and that was the end of it, they throve and were well-liking, became plump and delicate—and then were eaten on Martinmas Eve—and that was the end of it.

That was the end of it. For though the address sounded so lofty on Sunday, the geese on Monday were ready to recount to one another what befell a goose that had wished to make serious use of the wings the Creator had given him, designed for the high goal that was proposed to him—what befell him, what a terrible death he encountered. This the geese could talk about knowingly among themselves. But of course to speak about it on Sundays would be unseemly; for said they, it would then become evident that our divine worship is really only fooling God and ourselves.

Among the geese, however, there were some individuals which seemed to be suffering and grew thin. About them it was currently said among the geese, "There you see what it leads to when flying is taken seriously. For because their hearts are occupied with the thought of wanting to fly, therefore they become thin, do not thrive, do not have the grace for God as we have who therefore become plump and delicate."

And so the next Sunday they went again to divine worship, and the old gander preached about the lofty goal the Creator (here again the geese curtsied and the ganders bowed their heads) had set before the goose, whereto the wings were designed.

So with the divine worship of Christendom. Man too has wings, he has imagination. . . .[3]

Julian Nichols used this story in his sermon one Sunday. He did not act, however, like a common gander, using our divine worship to pretend to feelings that were not his. He spoke about holy movement in his life, but he gave equal time to the contradictions within him. "My life," he said, "is still a very fuzzy reflection of the fact that Christ died for me, knows that I exist, and cares for me in a personal way."

What kind of note is that for a preacher to make in a sermon on the Lordship of Jesus Christ? How can an inclusion of that nature help us to lift up limp arms and steady trembling knees? (Heb. 12:12 Jer.) The confessional note is probably a good example of what happens when a pulpit is given to a layman. Julian went even further. He told another story about a man who was climbing a mountain when he lost his balance and fell. Just as he was going over the face of the cliff, he grabbed hold of a frail little bush and hung on with all his might. Swinging there over the abyss he prayed,

> "Oh God, help me!"
> A soft Voice came back, "Do you trust me?"
> "You know I trust you, Lord. I'm praying to you."
> The Voice asked again, "Do you trust me?"
> "Yes, Lord, you know I do. Help me!"
> This time the Voice came back, "Then, let go!"[4]

Julian commented on the story:

> I am that man. I'm still hanging on like mad to the bush and I am staying away from the edge of cliffs in the first place. About as far as I've progressed is that I've ceased to worry about what tomorrow will bring. I've come to be excited just a little over what might happen. Whatever comes and however unexpected, I have to trust the Lord God, that it will neither overpower me nor be more than I can handle. I have faith that the place in Isaiah where God promises not to stamp out the smouldering wick applies to me as well as to the Israelites.

These words shed important light on how to take care of the moving center. If we are scared to death at the thought of moving out to bring a vision to fulfillment, we must not handle our fear by discounting our vision, or saying that it is impractical, or putting it down in all the other ways we know so well how to do. That is the way to quench the spirit and take light from the eyes. Far better to name one's fears—to make an honest statement. In the shadow cast by my own vision I hear myself saying, "I could do this or I could do that, but I am afraid of losing what I have and finding nothing important to replace it.

The vision may be of God, but I am not practiced in hanging over cliffs. If it is a matter of choice, I would rather not rely on God. I don't know him that well. I may not like the place where I am, but it is safe and familiar, and here I know how to cope."

If that is our confession we might think how we would go forward if we were to take a position of faith. Perhaps when all things are weighed, we too might be able to summon courage, and answer, "Here I am. Send me." If at first we do not find heart to move out past that place of safe return, we will at least know our true condition, and our vision will be intact. Our sincerity will enable us to be about the work of recovering wings and imagination rather than growing plump and delicate. One day our vision may grow so large that, despite our fears, we will find ourselves fully in its service.

In telling of his own condition, Julian described that place where many of us were in our lives, giving us help toward authenticity. He was also very direct about his own needs:

> So I stand here. I am aware that Christ controls what is happening. Christ controls our faith. I am also aware that Christ is confronting me; giving invitations that require answers. I need to go further, but I am up against internal resistance. In this situation I lay claim on you in this community. I need to be inspired by what you do, to be confronted and encouraged by you. In short, your love and your potential are very precious to me.

My thoughts drifted to a woman from South Africa, who had left her religious community after 13 years. She had secured the permission of her order to work with destitute people whose shanty homes were being destroyed by the practices of an oppressive regime. As the months went by it became clear that while the members of her community were willing to release her from her teaching assignment, they were no longer able to support her in the same way. They were not at fault. Response to call had taken her into land unfamiliar to them where their own energy and creativity were not flowing. "They were still a community," she said, "but they were not my community. They were unable to do for me what every community must do for its participants—challenge and encourage."

This is what Julian was saying in his own way, and it was good to hear. His words linger with me still:

"Your love and your potential are very precious to me."

The day seemed blissful. My friend needed not only my love, but he needed me to give serious attention to my yearnings, wild musings and other hints of untapped resources. And this for his sake—not for mine. Perhaps I was full of singing because I am so quickly saddened by the envy and jealousy of others, and cast into half-despair by my own. This well may be true of us all at one time or another.

This new in us which is seeking to emerge and to have a force and life of its own always meets with resistances in others as well as within ourselves. After Saul is chosen by God and the crowds have been dismissed, we have the line:

> Saul too went home to Gibeah, and with him went some fighting men whose hearts God had moved.          (1 Sam. 10:26 NEB)

Then we are given the other half of the picture:

> But there were scoundrels who said, "How can this fellow deliver us?" They thought nothing of him and brought him no gifts.
> (1 Sam. 10:27 NEB)

The darkness has always sought to overcome the light. Jesus was hounded from his birth to his execution, and what was done to him he said will be done to us. Envy and jealousy stalk our calls and visions.

> For Pilate knew it was out of jealousy that they had handed him over.          (Matt. 27:18 Jer.)

Around the crib of every new thought or idea are those who offer the gifts that will nourish and sustain, and those who withhold themselves, some who even seek the life of the new born. Whenever any grand plan or even a small venturing out is announced, we can count on the "nippers of buds" to be in the wings. They are usually not on stage—where their presence might be misinterpreted as the lending of support.

Envy and strife were common experiences in the early Christian communities. The reason then as now is that so few of us are obedient to our visions, and yet they never quite fade away. Although they may be out of sight, they make themselves known in a stab of pain, or a throbbing ache. When others talk of the buds they see or give attention to their visions, unfulfilled yearnings stir powerfully in us. Like every other hurting emotion, envy has information that is important for our life. This information does not lie outside us where our eyes and attention are fixed, but inside us where the pain is and where it is always hard to look. We are too practiced in turning away, and yet that turning away may be our unfaithfulness. We do not have to be afraid, for even though in our looking within we stumble on visions wrapped in grave clothes, Christ can raise them to newness of life. The dead can be unbound and let go.

When, however, we do not give attention to the new breaking forth in our lives, what others are doing will seem to diminish the significance of our acts. In the deeps of us we all know that there is something special for us to do.

The fear of desertion is another face appearing in the presence of the visions that other folk have. If we have abandoned ourselves, we are apt to cling to our friends and to fear that if they follow their calls we will be left more lonely. As we sense the Spirit resting on them, we grow apprehensive that they will be attracting a lot of human energy that might otherwise flow in our direction. Of course, this is the viewpoint of sin.

Energy flowing between human beings always produces more energy. When it is blocked and does not flow freely, we dry up and grow bitter. A person who has clung to what is high in himself knows this. Having spent himself on behalf of a vision, he finds returned to him a self whose company he enjoys. He is not threatened by others who follow calls and exercise gifts. In fact, he knows that community is dependent on each person's doing this. He yearns that what happened to him will happen to others. When Moses was told that the Spirit had lighted on others and that they had fallen into ecstasy in the camp, he replied,

"Are you jealous on my account? I wish that all the Lord's people were prophets and that the Lord would confer his spirit on them all!"                                              (Num. 11:29 NEB)

Our communities will know strife and envy unless we take with seriousness our own visions and become enablers of the visions of others. We do not have to worry that there may be a limit to the power of the Lord. Gordon summed it up in this way:

> The reality is that the newness breaking in you prepares the way for the breaking out of newness in me. The supply of God's love and creativity never gives out. All we have to do is be about the work of identifying the buds in ourselves and in our friends and thanking God that we know a little bit about His purposes for all human kind.

As we tend to our moving center—cultivate imagination, and give sanction to visions—can we make the assumption that all visions are of God? No, some prove not to be for their own time. They are not connected to anything deep in ourselves and do not mesh with anything deep in the hearts of others or any needs in the world. They quickly fade away.

In other instances, a vision may be the bearer of the new, but if uninformed by the historical, emotional and intellectual dimensions of a person's life, it will lack power. Many prefer to keep the faraway look in their eyes rather than to do the hard work of uniting heaven and earth within themselves.

Still other visions are demonic and must be brought to the light and crushed. Such was Hitler's vision of a superior race and nation. In his book, *The Mass Psychology of Fascism*, Wilhelm Reich suggests that, when a fascist character is seen puffing himself up, let him be asked quietly and simply in public:

> What are you doing in a practical way to feed the nation, without murdering other nations? What are you doing as a physician to combat chronic diseases, what as an educator to intensify the child's joy of living, what as an economist to erase poverty, what as a social worker to alleviate the weariness of mothers having too many children, what as an architect to promote hygienic conditions in living quarters? Let's have no more of your chatter. Give us a straightforward answer or shut up![5]

If Hitler were on the scene today he would probably be talking to the unemployed youth standing on our street corners, and perhaps to our assembly-line workers—the people to whom no one speaks, the ones who are never accorded preferential treatment, for whom no exceptions are made, and who are routinely treated as though their opinions are of no value. When you think about it, these are the ones that Moses would address. He might even tell them that they were a chosen people, a royal priesthood. The masses on the assembly lines of American industry are certainly in slavery to cruel pharaohs.

Barbara Garson's research for her book, *All the Livelong Day,* included two years of interviewing a representative group of assembly-line employees, as well as working with industrialized clerical workers and typists. She cites that some of these workers observed that they were given "less appreciation, less respect and less upkeep than the machines." She wrote:

> . . .The problem for management is that they must simultaneously suppress and yet rely upon human judgment. They need human beings and yet they fear human beings. They respond to that fear with an intensified division of labor and increasingly costly supervision. In the end they create jobs that are far too complex for robots but, on the other hand, far too regimented for chimpanzees. So they are stuck using human beings.[6]

In a speech, economist and author E. R. Schumacher raised the question, "How do we prepare young people for the future world of work?" Part of his own answer was that we should prepare them to be able to distinguish between "good work" and "bad work," and encourage them not to accept the latter.

> . . .That is to say, that they should be encouraged to reject meaningless, boring, stultifying or nerve-racking work where man or woman is made the servant of a machine or a system. They should be taught that work is the joy of life and is needed for our development; but the meaningless work is an abomination. . . .It is interesting to note that the modern world takes a lot of care that the worker's body should not accidentally or otherwise be damaged. If it is damaged, the worker may claim compensation. But his soul and his spirit? If his work damages them, by reducing him to a robot— that is just too bad. . . .

Schumacher's words seem too extreme, too counterculture, without the pictures Barbara Garson gives of legions of Americans trapped in the drudgery of meaningless work. Her book is full of examples like the keypunching operation where women sat side by side, unable to see each other or to move because their eyes and hands were kept occupied. To break their isolation they invented games on their machines:

On the older machines one had to hit harder and they made a louder noise. So we could hear each other and when we were doing the same job we could race. Sometimes we'd synchronize—we'd adjust so that we'd move into the next field exactly together. But we're always pressured to go the fastest with the least errors. So we'd synchronize for a while but it always turned into races. (In some keypunching departments each machine is wired to the supervisor's board. By watching the light on the board the supervisor could tell immediately when any operator in the room stops punching.)[7]

At a Ping-Pong factory in Rhode Island, Garson talked to a girl whose job it was to stack Ping-Pong paddles into piles of 50. Three other women took them off the stack and put tiny labels on the handles. The girl doing the stacking said:

Maybe it wouldn't have been so bad if I could have seen all the piles I stacked at the end of the day. But they were taking them down as fast as I was piling them up. That was the worst part of the job.[8]

Garson reports on the fastest assembly line in the world run by General Motors at Lordstown, Ohio, and manned by a work force whose average age is 24: At 101 cars an hour, each young worker has 36 seconds to perform his assigned snaps, knocks, twists, or squirts on each passing vehicle.

These atrocities affecting the human spirit are committed in the name of profit. According to Garson:

This way of organizing work is not the result of bigness, or meanness, or even the requirements of modern technology. It is the result of exploitation. When you're using someone else for your own purposes, whether it's to build your fortune, or to build your tomb, you must control him. Under all exploitative systems a strict control from the outside replaces the energy from within as a way of keeping people working. The humiliation and debilitating way we work is a product not of our technology but of our economic system.[9]

When will an Isaiah rise up to cry in the name of the Church,

"By what right do you crush my people and grind the faces of the poor?"                    (3:15 Jer.)

When will a human rights movement in America declare that management may not block the vision of its workers and reduce their days to routine and repetitious tasks, or act in ways that suggest to workers that they are tools for management's use? If the world's employers cannot institute changes in the name of justice, perhaps they can be moved to act in the service of their own future. When large segments of the population in every state are laboring under conditions that cut them off from love and knowledge and any meaningful sense of accomplishment, a mortally sick society is created. The only hope is that a people treated as slaves are also a people being prepared for rebellion. Part of the grandeur of the human spirit is that there comes a time when fear is cast out and the shout goes up, "Enough! I have had enough." The beginning of this can be seen in high absenteeism and sabotage by workers.

Now and then a worker declaring "enough" walks off his job to experience a worse form of oppression—unemployment. Of course, that is the fear that keeps any of us at a kind of work demeaning to our sense of self. The unemployed millions in the world would be glad to work at any job—never mind what it is. They want to feed their children, maintain their homes and spend their energy in labor, for the fact is that it is good to work. Next to our need for love is our need for work. Only those who do not labor at anything know the unspeakable ways in which human life is diminished when the right to work is denied. This is why retirement years prove disastrous to so many. They have nothing to do. Too often the retired find that they are not wanted and needed in the same way as when they were laboring at jobs with little encouragement for doing things that pull at the spirit. When leisure comes all those things that were waiting to be done seem not to be around—to have evaporated, as it were, into thin air. Maybe, after all, the suggestion of a vision tugging at us was only a brave word. Perhaps the visions that find no tilled soil waiting go away, or return to their origin. The poet wrote of the old, poor and mad shedding tears on their bitter bread, that even death passed them by.

> "They have never lived," he said.
> "They can wait to die."[10]

Such rejection seems to be a reality, but it is contradictory to the nature of God. He is the one who says, "...The word that goes from my mouth does not return to me empty, without carrying out my will and succeeding in what it was sent to do" (Isa. 55:11 Jer.).

But what of the unemployed, assembly-line workers, and those grown "too old" to be cherished as laborers? Are they not mocked by talk of visions? When all is said and done is not such talk only for that small minority, of which I am one, who, though they may dread finding themselves among the poor, are nonetheless people of option for whom the issue is one of nerve, or faith, rather than possibility? Perhaps, but who is prepared to settle for so limited a human view and one so contrary to God's own vision of a world in which young and old and those in slavery have had quickened in them the energy to make a different future? The new age will not be the achievement of an elitist group. The new age belongs to God.

I will pour out my spirit on all mankind.
Their sons and daughters shall prophesy,
your young men shall see visions,
your old men shall dream dreams.
Even on my slaves, men and women,
in those days, I will pour out my spirit.

(Acts 2:17–18 Jer.)

When Moses had his vision of a new society, he did not try to share it with the powerful and mighty, but with a slave people doing backbreaking labor. They were the ones open to believing in the schemes of madmen or God's men.

Does this then mean that only the poor are capable of participating in a "heavenly vision?" Not so, we who are rich are not necessarily lost. Moses was rich. The young man Moses reminds me of so many of today's youth. They seem to be in some kind of exile from their own houses of wealth and to be entertaining visions of a more just society. Despite the fact that they were born to the ruling class, life is not easy for them. They are full of troubles, and cannot find their way along the usual paths to success. Having identified the modern pharaohs, they do not want to join them. In fighting for a better way for the poor, they are fighting for a better way for themselves. Of course, some of them are doing nothing. They are standing immobilized—unable to buy into the existing structures of work, and unable to create new ones. They have visions, but do not take them with enough seriousness. The church seems to recognize only the call to the seminary and professional ministry, and to be strangely silent concerning other calls.

For help in understanding call and knowing whether it is of the devil or of God, we have to turn to the biblical people. Their experiences give us guidance in how to care for visions and to discern spirits. Saint Paul gives King Agrippa a brief and precise account of his own vision:

> "...Your Majesty, in the middle of the day I saw a light from the sky, more brilliant than the sun, shining all around me and my travelling-companions. We all fell to the ground, and then I heard a voice saying to me in the Jewish language, 'Saul, Saul, why do you persecute me? It is hard for you, this kicking against the goad.' I said, 'Tell me, Lord, who you are'; and the Lord replied, 'I am Jesus, whom you are persecuting. But now, rise to your feet and stand upright. I have appeared to you for a purpose: to appoint you my servant and witness, to testify both to what you have seen and to what you shall yet see of me. I will rescue you from this people and from the Gentiles to whom I am sending you. I send you to open their eyes and turn them from darkness to light, from the dominion of Satan to God, so that, by trust in me, they may obtain forgiveness of sins, and a place with those whom God has made his own.'"
>
> (Acts 26:13–18 NEB)

The gentle confrontation, "It is hard for you, this kicking against the goad," makes me wonder whether my own discontent might be resistance to the urgings of God that come to me in my wishes and sighs. I wonder also whether the address, "Rise to your feet and stand upright. I have appeared to you for a purpose," might be instruction that comes in every vision from God, if we could bend our ear and listen to the still small voice. We are in danger only when action, which is the dominant note of Scripture, is not in relationship with our being.

Paul told the king, "I did not disobey the heavenly vision." In fact, he explained that it was precisely for this reason he had been seized in the temple and his life threatened. He also let

King Agrippa know that he had God's help and that he was happy in choosing to be faithful.

> "I wish to God that not only you, but all those also who are listening to me today, might become what I am, apart from these chains."                                    (Acts 26:29 NEB)

We do not become servant and witness without a heavenly vision. The signs that a person is infused with God's divine essence are not hard to discern. When John was languishing in prison and beginning to doubt his own vision of a new age unfolding, Jesus sent him these joyous words:

> "Go back and tell John what you hear and see;
> the blind see again,
> and the lame walk,
> lepers are cleansed,
> and the deaf hear,
> and the dead are raised to life
> and the Good News is proclaimed to the poor;
> and happy is the man who does not lose faith in me."
>                                           (Matt. 11:4–6 Jer.)

Visions from God are integrally connected with justice for the poor, the sick and the oppressed, the lonely and rejected. They are concerned with love and beauty and laughter. They move us out to do a unifying work.

If we were each obedient to our visions the cities would have green spaces, birds in their trees, and architecture to quicken awareness of the divine life throbbing in the whole of the world. And the towns? The towns would have galleries to hold the works of their artists; theaters for the performing arts would spring up in their squares; scientists and poets would confer with each other; students would gather for debate and reflection, children would want to continue in life, and church congregations everywhere would be struggling "to make serious use of the wings the creator had given." Everyone would know what it meant to be the servant of the Most High.

Let us nurture the moving center in ourselves. Let us be faithful to our visions. Without them we perish.

*Elizabeth*

P.S. The following summary may be helpful to you in working with this letter:

1. The moving center will be nourished and cared for if we will each mount our own inner watchtower, and observe where the energy flows in us. What are our wishes? What are we sighing after?

2. When we have identified that place where the sap is building up, we are ready to begin the practice of letting the images come. This means giving up the direction of our thoughts— suspending all judgment. How do we see the new thing that we are doing or would like to do breaking from the bud? How does our vision unfold? Who are the people in it? Where does it send us? What places do we see?

3. If we were to believe our wild imaginings came to us from the Lord, what do we think that he might be trying to say through us?

4. What would our heavenly vision require of us who must deal with earth as well as with heaven? In the service of our vision what changes would we have to make in our lives? What would we have to let go? What would we have to embrace? Are we able unto these things? What are the images of our hopes? What are the images of our fears?

5. What are the resources that we offer to the fulfillment of what we see with our mind's eye? Are they adequate? Can we trust God to help? Is he the prime mover, or do we feel deep down that it is all dependent on us? If we were to act as though God had something to do with our vision, how would his direction, input and support come to us?

6. Write down the vision. If it delays, wait for it. From the *New English Bible*, another translation of Habakkuk's words:

> I will stand at my post,
> I will take my position on the watch-tower,
> I will watch to learn what he will say through me,
> and what I shall reply when I am challenged.

(Hab. 2:1)

## NOTES

1. "Blood of the Sun" in *The Collected Poems of Kenneth Patchen* (New York: New Directions, 1968), p. 328.

2. *Into the New Age* (Great Britain: Fontana/Collins, 1976), pp. 46–47.
3. Walter Lourie, *A Short Life of Kierkegaard* (Princeton: Princeton Univ. Press, 1942), pp. 235–234.
4. Source unknown.
5. (New York: Farrar, Straus & Giroux, 1970), p. xvi.
6. (Baltimore, Md.: Penguin Books, 1977), p. 219.
7. Garson, *Livelong Day*, pp. 154–155.
8. Garson, *Livelong Day*, p. 1.
9. Garson, *Livelong Day*, pp. 211–212.
10. Sara Teasdale, *Rivers to the Sea* (New York: The Macmillan Co., 1923), p. 63.

# 11

# ON
# CHILDREN
# IN THE WILDERNESS

*Dear Brothers and Sisters:*

Somehow it seems as though today's teenagers are in more trouble with their lives than the children of other generations. And yet, when I think of my own teenage years I have a certain envy for the visibility of their sufferings. I kept my own youthful griefs so private, perhaps because the adults in my world appeared to have troubles enough of their own. In those years of the depression, before a war solved our problem of finding work, I read about the girl and boy tramps of America who rode the freights across the country and lined up for soup in hobo camps. Though they captured my imagination, I never thought it was possible to join them, or to rage against parents for the turbulent household where I grew up.

In the close circle of my peers we all seemed busy trying to parent the needy grown-ups with whom we lived. Only much later did we learn that in trying to be parents we missed growing up ourselves. Is not this what so much of the pain of adult years is about—facing the hard fact that one has to stand on one's own feet while carrying about a heart that is still crying for the father or mother who will encourage, support, let us go and be there when we return?

We cast the husband, wife and friend in the role of parent and then complain against them when they do not measure up. We also promise ourselves that we will be better parents than our own, and learn too late that things are not very different for us. We did not honor our fathers and mothers enough to understand their sufferings, and to learn how those sufferings marked us. The only way any of us can make a fresh beginning is to acknowledge our hurt and to do the work of forgiving. Our shelves are lined with books that tell us how to be good parents. But when all the worthwhile advice is summed up it amounts to this: Enjoy your children and give them your attention—the two things we find it most difficult to do.

And where is the place that we can speak of how things go wrong between us and our children? Other families appear not to have our problems. At least we only hear about them when a child runs away, or takes her own life, or in some other way smashes herself up. All the rest of the time we share the stories of how well we are doing, creating a loneliness that only further divides us. We would all do better if we could confess the pain in our hearts, and use it to identify with all children in trouble. This would help us to take on the responsibilities of adulthood, to become adult ourselves and to encourage the young in the work of inward growth.

When a child is fourteen or fifteen we can no longer be the ever-present guides we might still long to be. Others will have to do for our children what we cannot do. But we can seize the moment of our relinquishment to give to other boys and girls what their parents might wish for them. The concept of the extended family is not modern, but a New Testament concept. When it is taken seriously, old walls come crumbling down, and a new, more just and peaceful world swings into view. This happened in 1965 for a few people from The Church of the Saviour community who caught a vision of what it would mean to create caring structures for the 900 abused and neglected children in the Washington, D.C. custodial institution known as Junior Village. Many of the babies in this public facility were lying almost motionless in their cribs—locked in the tearless, soundless despair of severe depression. Older children swarmed around every visitor with hungry pleas of "Hold me, Mama. Hold me."

The concerned adults who saw the miserable state of these children and heard their appeals organized themselves under the name of FLOC, For Love of Children. They were conscious of the fact that they were members of a liberation movement.

> Yes, I am well aware of their sufferings. I mean to deliver them out of the hands of the Egyptians and bring them up out of that land to a land rich and broad, a land where milk and honey flow. . . .
>
> (Exod. 3:7–8 Jer.)

In the words of Fred Taylor, FLOC's director, "Our call was to be a 'believing presence' in a city which was deaf, dumb and blind to any alternatives to the oppressive institution that it was maintaining for helpless children."

In the next two years FLOC was to make its cry of "let my children go," ring out in newspaper articles and sound in the palaces of the pharaohs. Time after time the group's leaders were to confront the hardened structures of the public sector that exercised a well-meaning but, nonetheless, cruel authority over their small charges.

Finally the sea parted—the bureaucratic pharaohs relented—and the children were moved back into the community to begin the next stage in their journeying toward a new land.[1] Junior Village was phased out of existence.

By then it became clear to everyone that only the first step had been taken. The children of the city would continue to need an advocacy people, if they were to have the protection and services they needed. Under FLOC's leadership all kinds of programs came into existence including a Wilderness School for boys. It was the residential camp for "problem boys" that I visited with Donna Nichols, a member of the FLOC program.

Most of the thirty boys in the camp have been referred through agencies or the courts. Some are on probation, others are boys whose parents "can't stand them any longer." Their distress is expressed in all forms of incorrigible behavior—irritability, loudness, screaming, walking out and staying away for three hours or three days, and fighting at home, at school, and on the streets. Their offenses range from petty thievery to grand larceny. They have not earned good marks any place. They are children who do not feel good about themselves—and probably never did.

On the way to the camp I recalled my own scant memories of the School's beginning when all was not going well. Somehow during that time the dream of a healing community where children in trouble with parents, schools and courts could work through their destructive behavior was not coming off. Concerned adults were discovering what Bruno Bettelheim had announced in the title of a book that "love is not enough."

One day the boys were so out of control that the director and counselors were on the verge of admitting failure. They brought their charges into Washington, D.C., so that they could meet with staff members of the FLOC central organization that is located on the third floor of the three-story Victorian house which is headquarters for the new communities of The Church of the Saviour. It was an agonizing day in which the leadership for the School debated whether to go on with the experiment or admit defeat.

When I went to my own office in the church building that day I encountered battered members of the camp staff huddled in conversation, nursing wounds that included black eyes and a broken arm, while here and there were youths opening soda pop, hanging out windows and sliding down straining banisters. Eight boys had managed to reduce a small army of adults to disarray.

Those of us who have been around The Church of the Saviour for any length of time know that the fulfillment of any project of enduring worth is always full of tears and agony, and accomplished by people who hang on in the face of obstacles that threaten to become overwhelming. The FLOC Wilderness School is no exception. Its actual site of 150 acres of woods bordering a national forest is near Front Royal, Virginia. But the real story is of adults and children not only carving out for themselves a place in this wilderness, but also treading an inner wilderness, wrestling with demons and angels to discover within themselves new territories on which to stand.

The School is the vision of Dabney and Alta Miller who had

spent three summers living with FLOC children on a farm in
Virginia along the Rappahannock River where Dabney was
raised. As they worked with these deeply hurt children, they
began to search for better ways to serve them. When the residential, therapeutic camp of the Salesmanship Club of Boys in
Texas was suggested as a possible model, the Millers set out to
visit the camp, which for twenty-six years had been working with
the problems of emotionally disturbed boys. They were cap-
tivated by what they saw and stayed on to work there for five
months.

When they returned home they had no trouble communicating the dream of a camp to serve troubled boys in the Washington area—not because visions of this kind are easily com-
municated, but because persons who are wholly committed to
giving those visions form and substance are always enormously
attractive. A support group formed aound the Millers. Doors
began to open.

Olaf Horneland, a dedicated Lutheran layman who wanted to
have his land serve others, offered the group the use of 150
acres of mountain property in Strasburg, Virginia. Mr. Horneland also owned a nearby motel which was about to be demol-
ished. Group members and friends set to work to tear it down
and used the wood and other salvageable materials to build a
dining hall at the new campsite.

"The money we needed," says Donna Nichols, "always came
through at the eleventh hour. No matter what the difficulty, it
was overcome. We felt that we were being guided." Such an
experience is shared by many persons and groups who set out
to do the impossible. The early days are graced, and the feeling
is that one's ways are campanioned. Then come the rocky times,
the times of God's hiding. Members of the School's support
group described those days in restrained words:

> In the Spring of 1972 the Wilderness School opened to a handful
> of boys and a mountain of trouble. How naive we were—to think
> that we could cope with severely disturbed youths! All hell broke
> loose and no one came out unscathed!

The troubled scene that I had come upon that day in the
Church gave hints of the scars and wreckage of the first months.

On that occasion, the group decided to continue, as they would so many times thereafter. The decision was made to return all but five boys to their homes. Later, after sending two more away, they began building the number back to seven, using new guidelines of selection. The program was still not working as it should. Too many stressful events riddled their days. They comforted themselves with the fact that they were learning, as indeed they were. Part of their capacity to endure was the conviction that they were being strengthened and prepared by their failures.

The hearing of their story reminded me of the response of author Corrie Ten Boom when an interviewer noted how her memories of life in a Nazi concentration camp threw a spotlight on problems and decisions we face here and now. "But this is what the past is for!" she said. "Every experience God gives us, every person He puts in our lives, is the perfect preparation for the future that only He can see."[2]

In his search for a person who could provide the experience that they lacked, Dabney turned to a boys' camp in North Carolina that had been spawned by the Texas group. Jerrell Bible, who was the group work supervisor at the North Carolina camp, joined them as the assistant director. He had no sooner arrived on the scene than a second rebellion broke out. This time all the boys were dispatched to ther homes, and the School was temporarily closed.

Once again the task of rebuilding was begun, and once again the School opened.

The staff put into effect a hard-won insight: A child himself would have to choose to participate in the program. The children interviewed were already being pressured by parents or other authorities to attend the camp. Some were threatened by the drastic alternative of a detention center. The counselors were committed to doing their part to make it easy for a boy to say "no," much to the dismay of parents who stood by.

John Mohr, the program's family counselor, said, "We are persistent in the asking of our questions. We bore in so that the youngster comes up with the real answers. The central question is 'Do you want to come here?' Anxious parents interrupt to point out 'The boy said he wanted to come.' But we state our question a number of times to ask in a variety of ways, 'Do you *really* want to come?' We begin in that first conference the process of teaching youths and adults to be honest in their feelings. The parents have been taught that loving a child is 'being nice' to him. They do not know how to be straight with a kid—to tell him 'You make me damned mad.' " What is repressed in the parents, as Carl Jung reminded us, comes out in the child, who in this case may be acting out the poisonous effect of repressed anger.

Though I had long wanted to see this camp that I had heard so much about, a deeper part of me was not fully anticipating the visit. Only recently had I learned to talk with so-called "normal" teenagers, and I did not expect to fare too well with these young exiles for whom the growing-up process had gone so far awry. The reading of their histories would alert any sensible person to the fact that these children would be indifferent, surly, or hostile—perhaps even cynical and calculating. After all, the mountain I was going to visit was inhabited by the famous "alienated young" who had demonstrated their ability not only to complicate their own lives, but also to give their elders feelings of inferiority.

The School's thirty boys were divided into three groups or tribes of ten each: the Mohawks, the Blackhawks and the Cougars. Learning that I was to be separated from Donna and sent off to spend the time before lunch with the Blackhawks filled me with no small degree of uneasiness. Two hours suddenly seemed like too much time to spend on any one mountain.

A young, attractive counselor who said his college major was psychology escorted me to the mountain tents of the Blackhawks. As we climbed the uneven path he caught sight of an anthill and bent down for a closer look. Having only the day before read that Konrad Lorenz was spending all of his Nobel prize money in observation of a few fish, I, too, kneeled to observe the ants. My guide commented that something unusual was going on. He pointed out pairs fighting here and there, numerous dead bodies, a few busily engaged in hauling off the victims, while others carried out less obvious activities. Before the day was over I found myself feeling the limitations of my own upbringing on city streets. Everyone in the camp seemed miraculously tuned in to the happenings of nature and to have

some kind of exquisite awareness that the mountain belonged
to more than humankind.

At lunch one boy said, "I used to want a box turtle and wished
that I could see one. Now they are all around." Then he added
"You can go out here and look under a rock and find out more
than is in a school book." He had either discovered or been
convinced that he was indeed learning and he took no small
pride in contrasting his accomplishments with those of contemporaries who were not so "set apart" or so especially chosen.

After we left the ants we met the Blackhawks on their way to
the showers. It was Homes Day, the once-a-month time of going
home for a weekend visit. The Blackhawks had changed the
schedule for showers and were taking theirs before lunch. We
went back and waited for them to finish, and then the counselor
asked for two volunteers to escort me back up the hill to the
tents we had never reached. My guides now were Billy, an elev-
en-year-old blond, and Mike, a taller, lean, black youth. Both of
them were handsome, soft-spoken and gentle, which made
them all the more engaging in this rough, outdoor setting. I
have since heard that a social worker who had read the records
of some of the boys and had then met with them wondered if
a mistake had been made and the information misfiled.

If these youths had any misgivings about relating to adults,
they did not show it. All their attention was bent on letting me
see all that was to be seen and on interpreting anything that
could not be "shown off." They explained how they had land-
scaped the sides of the mountain. Each of the Blackhawks had
taken trees from the woods and planted them in the campsite.
"We are responsible for the growth of our trees," they said.

On one older, more established tree was tacked the menu
plan for the week. At the bottom of the sheet was written, "80¢
a person." I had heard that the three tribes on this mountain
learned new math as they went about the business of building
lodgings, planning meals, shopping, cooking and doing all the
ordinary tasks of living, but it is one thing to hear about such
a concept of education and quite another to have it come to life
before your eyes, and to hear so convincingly in the conversa-
tions of children that it is working.

From the menu tree we walked to a new eating area that was
nearing completion, on to a small crafts center and then past

a log trestle on which ten toothbrushes were lined up, each in its place as though prepared for inspection. After that we went to sit on the "ready logs," a small square of logs set apart as the place of talking through problems. Whenever trouble arises between or among any of the campers, all ten gather on the logs with their two counselors, Chief Greg and Chief Bob, to deal with the conflict and any related issues. "Everyone sits quietly, then we talk, and we don't leave until our problems are settled." "How long might it take?" I asked. "All different times," they assured me. "Sometimes, way into the night. If we are not near the logs when an upset happens, we find a place wherever we are. When we were traveling to Texas, the driver pulled the bus over to the side of the road, and we sat there until we straightened everything out. In New Orleans we sat right down in the middle of the sidewalk. If we get into a hassle we don't go on 'til it has been settled."

These children were being taught what most adults have never learned—that it is possible to reason together when it is understood that feelings must be acknowledged and expressed, and when each person involved is committed to struggling for resolution. In these sessions there was time to justify one's own actions, time to listen to others express their feelings about an issue and time to receive important feedback not only from adults, but also from one's peers.

When we left the logs we moved to the "powwow" area. What is a powwow? Mike explained that "powwow is a time when everybody in the group sits around a fire at the end of the day right before we go to bed. We get to talk about how our day went, and how each other's day went. While someone else is talking about his day you may cut in if you have a good comment to make. After everybody has spoken the chiefs tell us how they think we did that day. By the time all that is over the fire has gone out, and it is time to go to bed."

Billy added, "We say how the day went. We also say how we want the next day to go. We talk about how much we are on our goals that day, and once a month we reflect on the whole month."

I asked him what his goals were. Unabashed, he replied, "Learning to control my temper, be obedient to authority and improve my math." I asked about the goals of some of the others in the group. Learning to handle anger and to deal with authority were pretty high on a list that included overcoming impulses to cheat, steal or run away.

Listening to them I wondered how such an exercise might be fitted into the structure of my own small group meetings, and I asked,

"Do you find powwows helpful?"

"At first it was boring—everyone saying the same thing."

"What makes a good powwow?"

"When you are truthful—when you tell the truth about yourself. When you have a good powwow you have a good next day."

I liked my young companions. We were treading similar roads that would seem strange only to those who are not walking this way. I was reminded of those guides who had helped me to define my own goals, and who had remembered that goals change and are replaced because they either become unimportant or have been achieved. I knew, too, that despite our similarities, Camus was right: "We are all special cases." Lou Ormont, a New York psychoanalyst, puts it in terms of opposites: "In the skin of differences we are all the same—relentlessly so."

But the wisdom of the youths caused a suspicious thought to cross my mind. Were they highly programmed children, saying words that had been said to them again and again? I tested the thought and rejected it. Surely this small community had, as every community has, a language to interpret its life for itself and for others. Furthermore, it had an authentic ring of being grounded in the experience of the campers.

My astonishment grew out of finding children working with concepts that at best only advanced adults are willing to implement. "Confess your faults to one another," James had written to the early church, ". . .that you may be healed" (James 5:16 RSV). But where are the households or the churches so bold as to work with so dangerous a teaching? The children were learning to be priests to one another. Of course, no one would put it that way. What they did say is that the boys who are there the longest are the best camp counselors for the new boys.

Not only are the boys learning to care for each other and to .

try out new kinds of behavior, but they are also learning to reflect on their lives and on the happenings of the day—the successes and the failures and how they came about. Maurice Nicoll, who was both author and spiritual director, wrote that a single day is a replica of the whole of one's life. "If a man does not work on a day in his life, he cannot change his life. . . ." Reflection is the art that every wise person extols, but since few ever teach or encourage that art, very little progress is made in the lives of individuals or civilizations. In the midst of adult relationships that are stable and genuine, these youths are learning to understand and direct upsurgings and intense feelings in themselves and to move toward some kind of commitment to goals that along the way will evolve into larger commitments to love and work.

John Mohr, who had been the principal of an elementary school for fifteen years or more before becoming the Wilderness School's family counselor, said, "The schools have nothing like this—nothing that comes up to the standard of helping kids with their problems, helping kids with the business of growing up." That growing up, as we all know, is negotiating the difficult passage between youth and adulthood when the ardent wish to remain forever a child can clash head-on with the equally fervent wish for independence and autonomy. Like every other new stage, adolescence is one of "tottering self-esteem" when the old has been shaken and the new is not yet. For all of us it matters who the people in our lives are at these crucial junctures, and for the young it matters greatly who the adults are.

The counselors, I learned, were painstakingly chosen for this extraordinary work of shepherding children in the slaying of dragons and the taming of wild horses. Always there were some twenty-five to thirty applicants for a job opening. The camp directors are aware that they are engaging a counselor for a period of close living that is not unlike a marriage contract. It is a twenty-four hour day for five days a week. Most of the time the staff live a goldfish-bowl kind of existence. The kids watch them closely, ferret out their weaknesses and play on them. On the other hand the kids will strive to follow their examples of strength, gentleness and integrity.

The director naturally seeks men who respond warmly to children, and men who, having faced and wrestled with their own problems, have as few internal conflicts as is possible for humans. Usually the counselors are psychology majors headed toward a lifetime of working with people and their feelings. Like the children, they will come out of the camp experience knowing themselves better and thus better prepared to guide others. They receive a week or two of training, but most of their learning is done on the job, simply because what there is to learn is not taught in schools. Some of them will not stay longer than a year, but the School administrators have come to accept this. "We don't sweat it. Give us a year's commitment," they say. "The important thing is that we always have good people who know what they are doing."

On this day the boys pushed back the tarpaulin of Chief Greg's tent to show off his living space and to point out what he had done to improve his living quarters, as well as what he had in mind to do. After that we made our way toward the site of the new latrine they were constructing. They explained that the old one was six feet deep, and that they were making the new one "eight feet and seven inches." The excavation was obviously a matter of some pride. The hole was already dug, and soon they would be building a tent for it.

Passing up a closer view of the latrine, we went on to the tent where Billy and Mike slept. Like all the other tents it had been designed and constructed by the boys. This one had four cots, four trunks, and a stove that would be the only heat through the winter months. Bobbie explained that the other boys in his tent were older than he, but that he did not enjoy being with children his own age. We sat in their tent awhile and talked about crafts and about possible careers they might choose. As we walked back down the hill to join the other Blackhawks for lunch, they decided I might be called Chief Elizabeth. I felt pretty good about that.

Lunch was not ready, so we joined the other Blackhawks and a chief to play charades. The children always included me with a natural spontaneity. They were obviously at a place of peace within themselves. Never the "outsider," I was now invited to take my turn playing charades. They gently urged me on, suspecting that my reluctance might be due to shyness. When they observed me brushing away the gnats they told me to raise my hand. "Gnats always attack the highest point of the body." Small and unexpected considerations are always welcome, but I was a stranger and the boys' inclusion of me seemed like extraordinary kindness, the more so because it was extended with so little self-consciousness.

At the noon meal the learning of math went on again in an unstructured and spontaneous way. A box on the table read "100% whole wheat." One boy inquired what that meant. When an explanation was given the children began indicating in percentage figures the amount of milk they wanted in their glasses. "Please fill it to 60%...100%...30%...."

I was always served first, and when it was time for seconds the last piece of meat was offered to me. Learning to be honest with their feelings, these children were also learning manners— learning that emotional honesty and openness are not the same as saying everything you think, or being unkind because you feel that way, both of which are deceptions which some leaders of adult groups set forth as psychologically sound principles.

After lunch the children scattered to complete preparations for their four o'clock departure for homes in Virginia, Maryland and the District of Columbia. One child named Jonathan remained with us in the dining room to wait for his parents who were due any moment. Not only was Jonathan going home, he was also scheduled for a conference with his parents and the staff. I had learned from John Mohr that these periodic conferences last from an hour and a half to five hours. Supervisors, parents and counselors are all there. The boy has come to know most of them well, and they encourage him to do the talking.

"We are consistently the advocate of the boy," said John. "We try to be as realistic as possible, supporting the kid to the hilt, though not always his behavior. We start off by letting him brag about himself—how he split a rail, or what he did on a trip. He has the same difficulty that any of us has in saying something self-building about ourselves. We let him know that it is all right, and we let parents see us confirming their sons. Most of them have forgotten or never knew how to encourage their kids.

Some of the parents have exacting standards for their child, and they continue to beat away at his already lowered self-esteem, without very much idea of what they are doing. It takes months and months to build the child up. We are sometimes starting from the ground level."

If counselors are successful with boys, they sometimes fail with parents. "We have a mother now who really hates her kid. She has left his father and married again, and the boy is in the way. For a child home is always the best place, but when a child is always receiving the message, 'you are not worth anything,' then his reaction is often, 'if I can't be good, I'll be bad.'"

Building a child's self-esteem is the main work of the camp, as it needs to be the main work of any of us who care about the future.

Jonathan was waiting for parents who felt that a son had been given back to them. "For this my son was dead, and is alive again; he was lost, and is found" (Luke 15:24 RSV). That kind of gratitude and appreciation is expressed by parents when they meet quarterly at the School, although it does not come right away for them any more than it does for the children. Like so many other parents today they have struggled too long with a sense of helplessness in the face of their children's problems. Teachers, social workers and courts have battered their own self-esteem, and they have small reason to trust this camp in the wilderness. Bit by bit, with the successes of their children, their own feeling of worth is restored.

When mothers and fathers gather at the School, the veterans of other seasons help the newer parents. At the last meeting a father from Roanoke, Virginia, was ready to take his child back with him. He was the only parent of the child and was a construction worker. Every time he made the 250-mile drive to the School for the required quarterly meeting it cost him a day's work. He was tired and angry and not at all sure the School experience was going to make that much difference for his boy. The other parents gathered around him to recount the progress of their own children in an effort to help him understand that the School was not a miracle worker. "Dealing with more than the surface problems of kids takes time, but it is worth it," was the loud and clear message. The father left without his son, but with a handful of stories to turn over in a perplexed mind and a small hope growing in a bitter heart.

As Jonathan waited for his parents he told us fragments of his own story. As a small boy he had been sent to live with an aunt because she was the best one to nurse him through a long illness. "When I came here," he volunteered, "I didn't trust any adult. I thought my mother sent me here because she didn't want me. Now I know she does."

The conversation did not mean that this thoroughly enchanting boy who would soon be going home for good would find his home carefree. Who of us ever does? On his trips home now he was surprised at sisters who quarreled and did not have any idea of how to settle arguments, and at a mom and a dad who ended their disputes by going to separate rooms. "I tell them to come out and talk about it," and they say, "Who does he think he is!" "They don't know how to put problems into a sea of forgetfulness," he states in a matter-of-fact way. Jonathan thinks he will be a veterinarian and a preacher, two posts that might assure him more attentive congregations.

One might yearn that Jonathan's path will lead him among people grown up in ways of relating. Perhaps, however, it is more realistic to hope that these children have been prepared to draw upon an inner strength when faced with homes and peers who might still consider the youths set apart—once by nonconformity and anger, and now by the peculiar experience of knowing about a sea of foregetfulness and how to be washed clean in its waters.

Driving home I worried some about Jonathan, and Billy and Mike, and their future in America. Would they be challenged by other institutions and ideals worthy of commitment? Or would the impact of homes, schools and society whittle away at their newly created selfhood? After all, they were still half in childhood, although they had, earlier than most, been working at the business of becoming adults.

My own reflections assured me that they had learned a lot about how to express themselves in a group—how to communicate with peers and elders and how to cope with some of their outraged feelings. Perhaps they were better equipped than most of us to handle the loneliness of perceptions that are not shared by one's friends.

Looking back on that brief morning at the FLOC Wilderness School, what I remember most vividly are none of the things that I have written about. I remember the faces of the children and how beautiful they were. I long to know that these youths are destined for good things.

Billy, Mike and Jonathan, may you flourish. May your Chiefs and your Tribes increase. And may each of you who has read this letter take a segment of your own vision and give it an incarnate life in the world.

*Elizabeth*

### NOTES

1. In secular terms, FLOC had mobilized small mission groups made up of three to eight persons. Each group had a specific task. Some recruited foster parents; some found houses for destitute fathers and mothers so that they had homes to which they could bring their children; other groups became a support system to foster parents; while still others worked to help natural parents get their children back from public custody.
2. Corrie ten Boom, *The Hiding Place* (Old Tappan, N.J.: Fleming H. Revell, 1971), p. viii.